Encounter

With

Oral Literature

Okumba Miruka

East African Educational Publishers
Nairobi

Published by
East African Educational Publishers Ltd.
Brick Court
Mpaka Road/Woodvale Grove
Westlands
P.O. Box 45314
Nairobi

First published 1994

ISBN 9966 46 691 6

Printed by
General Printers Ltd.,
Homa Bay Road, Industrial Area
P.O. Box 18001
Nairobi, Kenya
GO451

CONTENTS   PAGE

Dedication

This book is dedicated to my former teachers, Valerie Kibera, for her continuous personal support and encouragement, and Austin Bukenya, whose critical approach to literature has inspired me in my literary pursuits.

i

Preface

The writing of this text book began way back in 1984 with a simple seminar paper, "The Social Value of the Riddle – Luo Riddles as a Case Study". When the paper was presented from the 14th to the 16th of March, 1984, during Kenyatta University Creative and Performing Arts Festival, it received an enthusiastic response which encouraged me to expand the text into a longer document on riddles. The result in 1987 was a manuscript, "Insights into the Riddle" which was submitted to Heinemann Publishers and received a positive evaluation.

However, it was felt that the analytical approach used with riddles should also be used with other genres and further that the analysis of riddles would be more meaningful if done in the context of all other major genres. This meant going back to the drawing board and coming up with a text embracing the four genres namely riddles, proverbs, oral poetry and narratives.

Encounter with Oral Literature is essentially an analysis of these four genres. It takes off from the realisation that most oral literature texts in Kenya are anthologies and textbooks geared towards fulfilling the requirements of the secondary school syllabus. This text aims to excel that and introduce a discussion on analytical issues in the subject. Thus it focuses on matters of definition, terminology, classification, style and structure and social functions of the genres at a theoretical/analytical level.

The book sets to introduce, if not new knowledge, then a new way of looking at oral literature. This is particularly so with riddles and proverbs which have not received a lot of analytical attention locally in terms of classifying them and discussing their styles and social functions. The contention here is that these genres are as fecund for a full fledged analysis as oral poetry and narratives are. The other contention is that the four genres exist in a continuum rather than as disparate phenomena, what is referred to in the text as interfluence.

The book largely relies on oral literature from some Kenyan communities for analysis. But it occasionally uses material from elsewhere. It is hoped that the approaches suggested and the synthesis attempted will be enriching to other scholars and that this text will open a new vista for students, teachers and researchers at secondary school, college and university levels.

Okumba Miruka, 1994

PART ONE

RIDDLES

"If the mechanical acquisition of knowledge is of any value in the training of the mind, then it may be said that the learning of the riddle is important educationally."

J. Blacking in "The Social Value of Venda Riddles", *African Studies 20, 1961*.

What is a Riddle?

Riddles belong to the broad category of oral literature called the short fixed forms. This includes proverbs, puns, tongue twisters, idioms, euphemes and dicta. The distinctive features of these forms is that they are brief, compact and relatively invariable. In other words, they are short, compress a lot of meaning and remain relatively unchanged as they are passed on through generations. They are also called "formulae" by some scholars although that is a word which is used to mean other things as well in oral literature.

S.K. Akivaga and Asenath Bole Odaga in their book *Oral Literature: A School Certificate Course*, define riddles as "short sayings intended to make one use his wits in unravelling a hidden meaning"[1]. One could note from this definition the use of the word "saying" which, like "formulae", is used to denote other things, the most conventional being that a saying is a wise expression or what may be called an adage or aphorism.

Jane Nandwa and Austin Bukenya on their part define a riddle as "a word puzzle in which an object or situation is referred to in unusual figurative terms and one is expected to discover or decipher in literal terms what is meant"[2]. This descriptive definition specifies the content of a riddle as objects or situations, its style as figurative language and its import as the deciphering of hidden meaning.

A riddle as such is a short oral puzzle which presents the peculiar characteristics of a concept whether those characteristics are physical, behavioural or habitual and requires the unravelling of the concealed literal reference. The recipient of a riddle has to decode the literal reference and identify the concept meant. Let us take the example of a Luo riddle here:

> Challenger: *Mnaye* (Ready?)
> Respondent: *Kwithe* (Ready)
> Challenger: *Bura mochok etiend luanda.*
> A meeting convened under a rock.
> Respondent: *Yie tik.*
> The beard.

In this riddle, the beard is presented as a gathering of people and the chin as a boulder. The task of getting to the literal meaning makes one want to agree with Austin Bukenya who once said that a riddle is "a grain of wheat in a heap of chaff ".

When we look at the riddle again, we are bound to ask: exactly which part of the structure from the introduction to the answer is the riddle? And there are three possible answers. Basically, the riddle is the problem posed to be solved. This is confirmed when we consider that in some communities, the formula preceding the presentation of the riddle is "take a riddle". This is the case, for example, among the Agikuyu and the Akamba.

2

Secondly, the riddle may not be considered complete without the response. The answer must therefore be regarded as an integral part of the riddle. Thirdly, the preceding invitation, the response to it and even the procedure that follows should one fail to clinch the riddle the first time could also be considered part of the riddle. Bearing all this in mind, we could conceptualise a riddle as that whole structure beginning with the invitation and culminating in the right response.

Table of Indigenous Names of Riddles from Some Kenyan Communities

Community	Riddle	Riddles
Agikuyu	Ndai	Ndai
Luo	Ngero	Ngeche
Abaluhyia (Samia)	Omunaye	Eminaye
Kalenjin (Kipsigis)	Tangoch	Tangochik
Kalenjin (Sabaot)	Chetiangoe	Chetiangoet
Akamba	Ndai	Ndai
Maasai	Oloyote	Iloyetaa
Abagusii	Egetendagwiri	Ebitendagwiri
Pokomo	Kihodo	Vihodo
Taita	Ndawi	Ndawi

CLASSIFICATION OF RIDDLES

The classification of any material refers to the division and categorisation of such material into specific classes or groups according to some established and comprehensive criteria. It implies that there is a stock of material that needs to be differentiated. The categories developed should then be able to accommodate all manner of material considered. We can then talk of literary classification as a way of categorising, characterising, describing, typifying, identifying, grouping and labelling a given literary stock.

In literature generally, classification is done according to the *content* or *form* of the material. The content refers to the subjects, ideas, people, objects and situations presented in the work. Content classification deals with the "what" of the corpus. On the other hand, form classification deals with the "how". Form generally reminds us of shapes, patterns, appearances, dimensions and textures. Written literature comes to us in form of novels, short stories, poems and plays. They are in a graphic form. But oral literature comes in the form of narratives, poetry, riddles and proverbs. They are transmitted by word of mouth and therefore have an oral form.

But literature may also be classified using other criteria. In oral literature in particular, there is the sociological parameter i.e. where is the literature performed, when, why, and by who?

In *Oral Literature of the Maasai*, Naomy Kipury classifies Maasai riddles according to the objects referred to in the response. For example, she has the category "Riddles on Plants" under which she groups the following two riddles:

1. *Anaa ipi nabaa nimintieu atijing' a enkanasa olmakele?*
   Why are you so brave yet you cannot join the army?
   Ildupa.
   Because it is the sisal plant.
2. *Murran lainei kumok naa enkeju nabo eitasheyie.*
   I have many warriors all of whom stand on one leg.
   Olpopong'i.
   The Candelabra tree.

This approach to classification is found in many other texts including C. Chesaina's *Oral Literature of the Kalenjin*. Among the common classes found in the scheme are: people, natural phenomena, parts of the body, technology, material culture, domestic animals and insects.

A second method of classifying riddles is by the length. We could come up with two classes viz: those riddles uttered in one breath or single expressions and those delivered as a series of statements. The first category would have such riddles as:

Challenger: *Ushey jaran jidku dhaaf.*
  I left my smooth and nice stick on the footpath.
Respondent: *Mas.*
  A snake.

SOMALI

And in the second would fall such a riddle as:

Challenger: There was a mother with three children. She brought two oranges for them. But she wanted the youngest to get the largest share without annoying the other two. What did she do?
Respondent: She gave the oranges to the elder two and told each of them to give a piece to the youngest. They each gave her half an orange and she ended up with a full orange.

UNDIFFERENTIATED*

* The reference is used to mean those riddles that the author did not get an ethnic ascription for. Such riddles in this text were collected from an urban setting.

While we may easily call the first example a short riddle and the second a long one, we still have to acknowledge that there are riddles which may be delivered as single statements but which present a series of puzzles and by that virtue transcend the concept of being short. Here is an example.

> Challenger: *Nyatiende ariyo mobet ewi nyatiende ang'wen karito nyatiende ang'wen.*
> The four-legged sitting on the four-legged waiting for the four-legged.
>
> Respondent: *Paka mobet e wi mesa karito oyieyo.*
> A cat sitting on a table waiting for a rat.
>
> LUO

In order to surmount this kind of problem, what we referred to as short riddles could be called simple and the latter be called complex riddles. Kipury gives us an exposé of how this is done among the Maasai. She reveals that the simple riddles are characterised by:
- the opening formula *'oyiote'* (Are you ready?)
- stated as declarative statements rather than questions.
- are straight forward and are understood through memory.
- posed lightheartedly and with heavy reliance on literary aspects of humour, caricature and poetic licence with regard to ordinarily forbidden language.

The complex type, on the other hand, are:
- preceded by the formula *'Ira ng'en?'* (Are you clever?)
- presented as carefully-worded and systematic questions.
- solved by wit and reasoning.
- posed in a serious manner.[3]

Looking through Mwikali Kieti and Peter Coughlin's *Barking You'll Be Eaten*, we get yet another lead as to a possible system of classification. They classify Kamba riddles into four categories namely "incomplete statements", "onomatopoeia", "impossible acts" and "others".

An example of the incomplete statements is:

> Challenger: *Nesaa...*
> I almost...
>
> Response: *... kwosa nzoka ndĩmĩta mũnzyũ ngakũne ng'ombe.*
> ... picked up a snake thinking it was a stick to beat cows.

For onomatopoeia, they give:

5

Challenger: *Kungulu kangala kĩthembenĩ?*
'*Kungulu kangala*' in the drums.
Response: *Mũtwaano wa mbĩa.*
A wedding of rats.

And for the impossible acts, there is:

Challenger: *Ndũlĩsa mũtendeũ.*
You cannot climb this slippery one.
Response: *Mũthamba wa ĩĩu.*
A banana plant's stem.

Having briefly looked at the other schemes, the author proposes a stylistic-structural classification which groups riddles according to the form or structure of the challenge under four basic categories namely: Declaratives, Interrogatives, Epigrams and Phonologues.

Declaratives

Most riddles are statements. The challenger presents a description and the respondent is expected to work out or guess the object or situation referred to or described.

These statements are declarations of the characteristics of the concepts e.g.

Challenger: *Mũthigari ahĩtũka na tai*
A policeman has passed through in a tie.
Respondent: *Ngigĩ.*
Grasshopper.

GIKUYU

For a memorable name we classify them as *declaratives*.

Whereas many riddles can be classified as declaratives, within the class, more subdivisions can be done upon closer scrutiny of the riddles. The above riddle is a straight description of the grasshopper as possessing the inner membraneous wings which resemble a tie. We can categorise such riddles more specifically as **descriptive declaratives**. There is another sub-category which displays other interesting features.

Here is an example:

Challenger: *Ngwate kisithe natuithi.*
Catch my tail and we go.
Respondent: *Iembe.*
The jembe (hoe).

KAMBA

6

In this riddle the relationship of an object (hoe) and space (land) is presented. If digging has to take place there must be action involving the digger, the implement and the land. Isolated, they are redundant. Likewise, if a rat is to be trapped, it must interfere with the trap. It catalyses its own trapping and is therefore as much responsible for it as the trap. Similarly, a person who gets a thorn in the sole of his feet has actually stepped on the thorn. It is like the thorn is only repaying the assault, by lodging itself in the victim's sole. These two ideas are summarised in the riddle below.

> Challenger: *Tega nikutege.*
> Trap me I trap you.
> Respondent: *Mwiba ama mtego wa panya.*
> A thorn or a rat trap.
>
> SWAHILI

Such riddles present us with a give-and-take kind of situation. One object reciprocates the action of the other. We will call this sub-category *reciprocal declaratives*.

But one may also talk of such riddles as presenting the relationships of objects over space and indeed call them spatial riddles.

Interrogatives

Basically all riddles are questions. But some are explicit while others are implicit. As in the declaratives, the question is implied. In order to differentiate them from the more explicitly inquisitive riddles, we call the latter interrogatives. Here is an example:

> Challenger: *Eshiitsanga munzu nishi?*
> What is bouncing in the house?
> Respondent: *Eshimuka shia amabeere.*
> The churning gourd.
>
> ABALUHYIA (Batsoto)[4]

What must be noted is that the presentation of a riddle as a question or a statement could largely be a matter of choice. For example, the foregoing riddle may also be posed declaratively viz: "I am bouncing in the big house". In fact, in actual riddling, there is a liberal interchange of declarative and interrogative forms of the same riddle. This happens when the response to the riddle is slow in coming hence prompting the challenger to reissue the riddle. Something like this may happen:

> Challenger: *Pastola ungu wa kitanda.* } Declarative
> A pistol under the bed.
> Respondent: (Delay)

7

Challenger:	*Pastola ii niila yi ungu wa kitanda?*	
	What is this pistol under the bed?	} Interrogative
Respondent:	*Mai ma nguku.*	
	Chicken's droppings.	

KAMBA

In such a case, one has to consider the first rendition for purposes of classification or otherwise adopt a descriptive approach of the whole riddling activity as we have done.

Epigrams

These are riddles which present a series of puzzles within one. Such riddles display a distinct poetic and discernible (often numerical) correspondence between the challenge and the response. To illustrate, there is a Luo riddle we have used before:

Challenge:	*Nyatiende ang'wen mobet e wi nyatiende ang'wen ka rito nyatiende ang'wen.*
	The four-legged sitting on the four-legged waiting for the four-legged.
Response:	*Paka mobet e wi mesa karito oyieyo.*
	A cat sitting on the table waiting for the rat.

This riddle relies on creating the impression of so many four legs. The number 4 is the base of comparison of the objects vis-a-vis the positions of the objects. Arithmetically, we can map the first four legs to the cat, the second to the table and the third to the rat. This kind of linear comparison makes the correspondence direct and analogical. In this text, we classify such epigrammatic riddles as **analogues**.

The second type of epigram is longer and has a question at the end. It has a series of statements or premises upon which the question is based. This kind of riddle does not entirely depend on memory. For example:

Challenge:	One day I sat on a cliff and started playing with the dry pepper my mother had sent me to fetch. Some of the pepper fell into cracks in the cliff as I was playing. Since the cracks were too tiny for my fingers to get into, how did I remove the pepper?
Response:	You poured water into the cracks to float the pepper which then made it easy for you to retrieve them.

MIJIKENDA

The most significant feature in such riddles is that they require the respondent to think up a logical answer by puzzling out the clues given. Because of the detective knack that

8

unravelling the clues requires, such riddles may be called **sleuths**. Thus we end up with two sub-categories of epigrams: *Analogues* and *Sleuths*.

Phonologues

These are riddles which use sound to imitate and portray the behaviour, characteristic quality of the object, and situation of idea referred to. For example the Agikuyu have a riddle *"Hīī"* to mean darkness. Also the Luo will say:

> *Hurr lokani hurr lokacha*
> Hurr this way, *hurr* that way.

The answer to this riddle is "Night runner". The sounds "hurr" imitate the roughish way of night running and accompanying acts and noises at night. For the same concept of the night runner, the Wanga sub-group of the Abaluhyia community have the riddle:

> *Huyu huyu paaa*

which simulates how the night runner wields and swings a stick in the air to scare people at night.

Riddles which imitate sounds are usually called ideophones i.e. we get the "idea" from the "sound" (phone). Like we did with riddles which have direct arithmetic correspondence, we shall here call ideophonic riddles with another name: Phonologues, a term first used in L. O. Sunkuli and Simon Okumba Miruka's *A Dictionary of Oral Literature* (Heinemann Kenya, 1990).

STYLE

Being part of oral literature, riddles are primarily oral. Analysing the style of oral art necessitates looking at the aspects of performance or rendition as well as the literary structural aspects.

Performance

The performance of riddles requires at least two people: one to pass the challenge and the other to respond to it. The one who offers the challenge may be called the challenger or proposer and the other one who responds the respondent. These positions are not fixed, however, but are interchangeable such that after posing the riddle, the then challenger becomes part of the respondents and someone else becomes the challenger. Because of this procedure of rotation and the shortness of riddles that makes it possible to go through many riddles at one sitting, we may not talk of an audience in riddling since no one in the group is expected to play a passive role without participating in challenging and responding.

But there could be exceptions. For example, among the Somali, adults sit aside in a group and listen to the children riddling and correct them where necessary.

In some communities, before riddling begins, there are certain fixed utterances to announce the session. Among the Mijikenda of the Coast Province, for example, the riddling session begins with one posing the challenge announcing: "Let's tell riddles and see who can answer more than the others". Then the riddling begins.

Among most communities, each riddle is preceded with an opening formula. Let us take some examples from two communities.

The Basoga of Uganda introduce the coming riddle by saying:

Challenger: *Kikoiko* (which means riddle).
Respondent: *Kidhe* (Let it come).
Challenger: *Kikoiko*.
Respondent: *Kidhe*.

The Kipsigis of Kenya, on the other hand, say:

Challenger: *Tangoch?* (May I say a riddle?)
Respondent: *Ichot* (Say it)

What are the functions of these formulae? Take the Mijikenda formula for instance. The utterance "Let us tell riddles and see who can answer more than the others"; 1) sets the mood of the occasion as that of competition; 2) terminates the ongoing activity and directs the mind to the world of riddling; 3) calls upon the participants to take the activity seriously and therefore motivates them; 4) defines and identifies the challenger from the rest of the group (i.e. the first person to say the formula indicates he/she is ready to offer a riddle and so all the others attend to him; and 5) announces the coming of the riddle.

After the formula, the riddle is presented and the respondent offers an answer. Should the respondent fail to get it right, another one tries and so on. Among most communities, if all fail to get the correct response, a theoretical prize is given to the challenger. In the Luo community, a male challenger will ask for a bride and the female challenger will ask for a groom for a mock marriage. The Abaluhyia ask for a bride, the Agikuyu for land or cattle, the Kipsigis for land and the Mijikenda for a town.

It might also be noted that the acceptance of the prize differs from community to community. The coastal peoples always accept the given prize of a town. This has got a socio-cultural background that we shall discuss later. The Luo, on the other hand, will not just accept any prize. Once offered a bride or groom, the challenger may decline the offers until his or her desire is met. The respondent will in the meantime be naming "spouse" after

10

"spouse". This offers a very interesting interlude in that the respondent may not immediately name the person that the challenger is known to have friendly feelings towards. Instead, he or she will offer those people the challenger is not known to be very fond of. As soon as the solution is given by the challenger after the prize, another person takes over and poses a riddle starting off with the introductory formula. The Somali do not give prizes but the defeated respondent will say: *"Maaqaan"* meaning "I do not know". At this confession, the challenger rejoices by saying *"Waankaahelay"* meaning "I have scored" and then gives the answer.

In summary, one could say that riddling takes the following general pattern:

Part One

The challenger or proposer invites.
The respondent agrees to take the riddle.

Part Two

The challenger poses the riddle.
The respondent offers an answer.

Part Three (If the response is wrong).

The challenger asks for a prize.
The respondent makes a prize offer.
The challenger accepts the prize.
The challenger gives the correct response.

The process could be summarised diagrammatically as in the following concentric cycle:

The Riddling Cycle

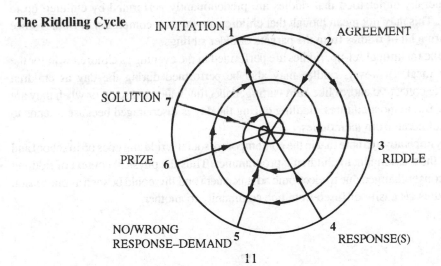

11

The cycle represents all possible riddling stages. The outermost circle stands for all the participants. The concentric ring starting from the point of invitation indicates the challenger who becomes the centre of attention as soon as he utters the formula. Thus he moves to the imaginary centre of the group. When his riddle has been solved, he springs back into the outermost circle as represented in the second diagram below. All the arrows pointing to the outermost circle indicate the activities of the challenger. The others represent the respondent's activities.

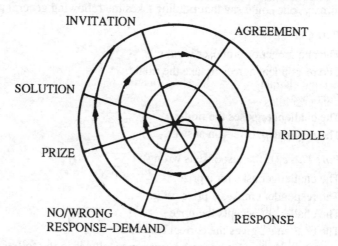

But who performs riddles, where and when?

It is generally understood that riddles are predominantly performed by children up to teenage. This may not mean though that children are the sole composers of riddles since they learn a lot of riddles from the parents or older siblings.

In the traditional set-up, riddles are performed in the evening as children wait for the evening meal. However, riddles may also be performed during the day as children undertake collective chores like baby-sitting, collecting water and so on or when they are playing. But in most cultures, riddling during the day is discouraged because it tends to distract children from their duties.

It is imperative to note that in the contemporary society, riddling goes on in school and through the mass media in children's programmes. Thus the physical context of riddling has obviously changed due to electronic advancement and this could be seen as one reason why riddles get easily diffused from one community to another.

Structure

In order to broach the question of structure, we will remember that we defined a riddle as "a short oral puzzle which presents the peculiar characteristics of a concept be they physical, behavioural or habitual and requires the unravelling of the concealed literal reference". In a wider context, the riddle belongs to the class of discourses we have called the short forms or what another scholar, Roger Abrahams[8], refers to as the simple forms.

As we said earlier, the short forms are characterised by their shortness or brevity, compactness and fixedness. A riddle such as the Agikuyu *"Ihuu"* to which the answer is "pregnant woman on a hill" simulates the sigh of a pregnant woman going up a hill. The riddle consists of one sound word which signifies a specific concept in the community. Furthermore, in the Gikuyu language, the sound word itself means pregnancy.

There are, of course, some more elaborate riddles. But they are still accommodated by the definitional characteristic of brevity. An additional element that can be noticed in some of the longer riddles is that they pretend to tell stories and have typical openings such as "there was ..." This gives them a narrative structure.

In analysing the structure of a riddle and after acknowledging that a riddle is laid out in two units, the descriptive elements (the challenge) and the referent (the response), according to Robert A. Georges and Alan Dundes[9], it is also important to look at these elements closely. Doing this means considering the question of imagery and language use.

Charles T. Scott observes that the language and content of riddles "tend to focus predominantly on concrete, homespun details rather than on the more abstract features of human relations and behaviour which one expects for instance, in proverbs and aphorisms"[10]. Scott's point, put another way, is that riddles derive their imagery from the immediate surrounding of the community and that both the descriptive elements and the referent are tangible. But this may not always be the case as we shall illustrate later that riddles may also deal with very abstract concepts.

At this point, it may be noted that most riddles are in fact metaphors. For example, there is a Swahili riddle:

> *Mwarabu kavaa kilemba.*
> An Arab wearing a turban.

The answer is:

> *Kigunzi.*
> A maize cob.

The maize cob is here presented as if it were an Arab. And the metaphor goes further by ascribing to the cob the aspect of being dressed hence making the reference a personification.

Another type of image we find in riddles is *apostrophe*. Apostrophe means addressing an object that is absent or dead as if it were present, alive and could respond. An Agikuyu riddle for example says; *"Mūthūngū kumerera"* (Whiteman crawl) to which the response is *"Ndogo"* (Smoke). This is in an intimation of a conversation with the whiteman.

It could be noted that this riddle is not just denotative of smoke. It is also a vent through which the community gets back at the colonialist. History tells us of the subjugation of the African by the whiteman. Things changed when the African countries fought for and regained their independence, an occurrence that supposedly turned tables on the colonialists and put the African at par, politically, with the colonialist.

The tone in the riddle could be called confrontational. This is a significant characteristic of riddling and one that inheres in the activity of pitting the challenger against the respondent. Abrahams describes the atmosphere as one in which "the spirit of licence reigns allowing for a play off of motives we don't allow ourselves under the circumstances of real life"[11]. Thus riddling accords one a chance to abuse and be abused without taking offence. And thus we get such egocentric riddles as the Kamba one:

Challenge: *Nikanini lakini mwenyu ndakasinda kuuwa.*
              A small married woman who cooks better than your mother.
Response: *Nzuki.*
              Honeybee.

Obviously, the challenger here is taunting the respondent by claiming that the respondent's mother is a lousy cook. The insult motivates the respondent to at least get the correct response by which he would be intimating that it is actually the mother of the challenger who is such a lousy cook. We get many such riddles which take the first and second person singular to introduce the competitive element.

Many riddles also exist in balancing parts. For instance the Batsotso will say:

Challenge: *Endi hano khandi endi yilia.*
              I am here and I am there.
Response: *Eshiinini.*
              The shadow.

As it were, the first part "I am here" balances with "I am there". This structural aspect of existing in balancing parts is called parallelism.

To conclude this section, we need to look at the mnemonic facility that riddles use by considering the rhythm of riddles. Riddles are stylised expressions that lie between speech and song. By their very nature of posing challenge, they require fast delivery. When they are not expressly sung, as occurs in a number of cases, they are spurt out.

In order to achieve the mnemonic effect, riddles are inlaid with *alliteration* (successive repetition of a consonantal sound in words coming close together), *assonance* (successive repetition of a vocalic sound in words coming close together in a statement) and *ideophones*. Let us take an example to illustrate from this Luo riddle.

> *Ding didi di di di ding didi*

The response is:

> *Wach mandas momiyo opad lemba*
> It is because of buns that my cheeks have been slapped.

The riddle is essentially sung in its challenge and response. We notice the alliteration of "d" and the assonance of "i". We also notice that there is a symmetric correspondence between the sounds in the challenge and the syllables in the response viz:

> Ding didi di di di ding didi
> 1   2 3 4 5 6 7   8 9
> Wach mandas momiyo opad lemba
> 1   2   3   4 5 6 7 8 9

Such effects enhance the rhythm and aesthetics of the riddle.

SOCIAL FUNCTIONS OF RIDDLES

What social functions do riddles fulfil? Are riddles just pastimes or do they have some inherent messages to convey? How do they respond to environmental, historical e.t.c. changes? These are some of the questions which we will examine, directly or indirectly, under this section sub-divided into:

- A. Overture
- B. Environmental Education
- C. Pedagogy
- D. Cultural Norms
- E. Social Commentary and Entertainment
- F. Record of Change

Overture

A critical analysis of oral literature reveals that the different genres are highly interrelated. In any one community, we may get a narrative, riddle, poem and proverb springing from the same idea and based on the same theme. This interrelationship even goes beyond geographical boundaries. This section posits that this interrelationship exists in a continuum in which the riddle is the first in the series. It also relates this to the fact that in many communities, riddles are performed before narration commences as some kind of appetizer. This is particularly important because in riddles, there are a cross-section of objects, situations, experiences and ideas that narratives try to explain in broader space. At the physical level, there are the birds, insects, other animals, utensils, landscape, weather e.t.c. that riddles characterise and prepare us to appreciate in narratives. See the following riddles.

Challenge: *Omunani kwanje kuyanzisinjia boosi.*
My coconut entertaining the world
Response: *Eliuba.*
The sun.

LUHYIA

Challenge: *Endi nende omukunda kulimo ebisichiri bibiri ebikhongo nende ebinji ebititi.*
I have a farm with two large stumps and several small ones.
Response: *Eliuba, omwcsi, nende tsinginini.*
The sun, the moon and stars.

LUHYIA

Challenge: *Mũgũnda wakwa ũthiũrũkĩirio ni mũthigari ũmwe.*
All around my farm there is only one policeman.
Response: *Mweri kana riũwa.*
The moon or sun.

GIKUYU

Challenge: *Timũthaka arĩ na nguo ta arĩ njaga.*
When dressed, she isn't as beautiful, as when naked.
Response: *Mweri.*
The moon.

GIKUYU

Challenge: Present at day, absent at night.
Response: The sun.

UNDIFFERENTIATED

Challenge: I have one eye but I see everywhere.
Response: The sun.

UNDIFFERENTIATED

16

In the above riddles, the sun is shown as a patron of space. From science we know its importance to both plant and animal life. It facilitates photosynthesis and supplies human beings with light, heat and vitamin D. By appearing at day and disappearing at night, it regulates our daily life patterns. Together with other climatic factors like rain, the sun determines farming seasons. Therefore, it is a kind of a master. The image of an entertainer portrays it as being impartial and accessible to everyone.

The sun, moon and stars are given as crops in a garden. We cultivate and get crops from farmland. Here lies the idea of provision and the sustenance of life. Again, the sun and moon are presented as policemen. People perform all sorts of evil in darkness. Any kind of light is therefore a protection against many ills that could easily occur. Sunlight and moonlight thus offer natural security. On the moon is the frequent association with beauty. It is not surprising that moonlight is universally associated with romance; its soft illumination creates an emotive and pacifying atmosphere.

Narratives in which the sun, moon and stars appear are dominantly concerned with the origin of life and death. The riddles as such categorise their connection with life physically and readies the mind for understanding their mythical role in the narratives and poems.

In a Luo myth on the origin of death, moon (a deity), grew concerned about the epidemic death of mankind. To rectify the situation and make man immortal, moon sent word that man should present him a spotlessly white piece of fat. Man slaughtered a ram and extracted the fat which he then gave to chameleon to deliver. The latter, being as clumsy as he is, soiled the present and when he reached moon, the moon rejected the token and ordered: "Tell man that because of his impudence, he shall continue to die and never rise again as I do". That is why man dies and never resurrects, according to the Luo myth.

The significant thing here is the apparent immortality of the moon. It appears, disappears and reappears in different seasons. Even if it is not there now, we know it is definitely coming another time. Below are poems from different African communities on the same theme and expressing the interrelationship of the celestial bodies.

Prayer to the Moon[12]

Take my face and give me yours
Take my face, my unhappy face
Give me your face
with which you return
when you have died
When you vanish from sight.
You lie down and return –
Let me resemble you, because you have joy

You return evermore alive
after you vanished from sight.
Did you not promise us once
that we too should return
and be happy again after death?

BUSHMAN

This poem is a eulogy. It praises the beauty, joy and eternity of the moon while re-emphasising its association with life.

The Sun[13]

Where are your children, sun?
Where are your children?
As you have eaten all your own
why do you chase the moon
to take her children for your own?
You can never succeed –
go and look for your own.

EWE

The Sky[14]

The sky at night is like a big city
where beasts and men abound
but never once has anyone
killed a fowl or a goat,
and no bear has ever killed prey.
There are no accidents; there are no losses.
Everything knows its way.

EWE

In *The Sun*, sun is shown as an aggressor on the lesser moon. Their day and night alternation seems to be a race where the sun is vying for moon's children – the stars. This poem is comparable to the riddle that depicts the sun, moon and stars as inhabitants of the same garden.

Challenge: I have a farm with two large stumps and numerous small ones.
Response: The sun, moon and stars.

LUHYIA

The riddle compares the sizes, the poem their presence in connection with times of the day. It is like the sun chases away the moon as day comes and the moon chases away the sun as night comes. Knowing a bit of astronomy, we can see that the sun is a star and is seeking to reunite with its brothers which the moon has apparently taken away by virtue of appearing together at night.

Let us now take the inter-genre relationship across the regions.

Challenge: *Irio njega cia mwana.*
Best food for a baby.

Response: *Toro.*
Sleep.

GIKUYU

Challenge: *Sixir geed-kaasootuur.*
Witchcraft throws you out of a tree.

Response: *Hurdo.*
Sleep.

SOMALI

Sleep is one of man's basic needs alongside food, clothing, shelter and sex. If the body is denied sleep, it compensates automatically through dozing, and if denied that, eventually breaks down. According to the Gikuyu riddle, sleep is therefore symbolically a nourishing food. The Somali riddle puts it even more humourously as an invincible conqueror. Among the Luo, the same feeling is expressed in the saying: *"Nindo tek matero janeko"* meaning "sleep is so strong, it overcomes even the lunatic". The Agikuyu live in the central part of Kenya, the Somali in the eastern and north-eastern parts and the Luo in the western part. Yet we can see a similarity in thought with regard to sleep. Going outside Kenya, we get the same idea expressed in the following poem.

The Sweetest Thing[15]

There is in this world something
that surpasses all other things
in sweetness.
It is sweeter than honey
It is sweeter than salt
It is sweeter than sugar
It is sweeter than all
existing things.
This thing is sleep

19

When you are conquered by sleep
nothing can prevent you
nothing can stop you from sleeping.
When you are conquered by sleep
and numerous millions arrive
millions arrive to disturb you
millions will find you asleep.

SOUSSOU

Earlier on, we stated that riddles are performed prior to narratives and they mention objects referred to in greater detail in narratives. An example will show this relationship.

Challenge: *Khupa omulosi namwale nase ndimbe.*
               Whistle at the other end and let me sing it.
Response: *Ochore.*
               The parrot.

LUHYIA

This riddle states the magnetic ability of the parrot. In Orature, birds are known to relay messages especially advising the heros or heroines and commenting on the events as a moral or objective voice. In this way, the narrative acknowledges birds as useful companions to man and this symbolises the ideal interrelation of man and his environment. The birds in the narratives differ from community to community. Common examples are the doves, weaver bird and the chaffinch, called *Hundhwe* among the Luo. After the riddle has stated the bird's ability to reproduce words, it is automatically understood when the same occurs in the narrative.

In *Keep My Words*[16] by Onyango Ogutu and Adrian Roscoe, there is the story of Magundho, who goes to visit her boyfriend, Obong'o. She is accompanied by her sister Awuor. Obong'o and his mother, who are witches, hypnotise and carry her out to the bush not knowing that Awuor, who is awake, follows them there secretly and drags her sister to safety. After some weeks, Obong'o meets Magundho on her way to a village dance and kills her. The bird Hundhwe is on standby to witness this slaughter. It flies to the dance arena and reveals the murder, naming the villain who gets very embarrassed. Finally, it leads the dancers, now mourners, to the scene of the tragedy and the grave. The corpse is unearthed and taken home. Hundhwe is rewarded with cattle for this gracious act. From this, we learn that the bird not only has speech abilities, but symbolises conscience also.

In the foregoing discussion, one point is that riddles bring to us objects within the environment that we encounter in daily life and which also appear, often starring, in narratives e.g. chameleon, birds, insects, cattle, rivers, forests, human beings, plants, domestic utensils and industrial tools. At the second level, the riddles give us initial insight to perceive and appreciate their symbolic roles in narratives. The primacy of the riddle to the narratives, poetry and proverbs makes it an introductory genre. This introductory function in preceeding narration and identifying the objects we encounter in the other genres makes the riddle an overture

Environmental Education

Riddles stem from observation and comprehension of the environment. The environment should be understood as the totality of the physical, biological and socio-cultural surroundings within a given place. Since each community occupies a specific geographical area, their riddles differ in content. Each community uses the objects within its environment in its art. This is what may be called "immediacy of derivation".[17] As such, an agricultural community will constantly have riddles referring to crops. Let us take some apt examples:

Challenge: *Nikanini mwenyu ndakasida kuua.*
A small married woman who cooks better than your mother.

Response: *Nzuki.*
The honeybee.

KAMBA

Challenge: *Obambo rachoke.*
Obambo the bony.

Response: *Pikipiki rachumbe.*
Motorcycle the metallic.

LUO

Challenge: *Hashaydu ayadea geela ugu gaaben geedahana boarkey kadaaqda.*
My camel is the shortest but it eats the tree at the top.

Response: *Shimbirta.*
Bird.

SOMALI

Challenge: When I slaughter my cow, I don't throw away anything. I eat everything including the bones.

Response: The coconut.

MIJIKENDA

In Kenya, Kambaland is famous for production of honey. It is therefore not surprising that the Kamba people have a riddle based on the honeybee. The Luo on the other hand are

21

associated with riverine and lacustrine surroundings. Fish is common in their diet. "Obambo" is the tilapia that has been split and then sun-dried. The splitting exposes its midrib bones and hence makes it appear bonier than other fish. The exposure of the bones offers a good comparison with the spokes and other metallic gadgets in the motorcycle.

The Somali live in the north-eastern and eastern parts of Kenya. These are arid and semi-arid areas characterised by nomadic lifestyle. It is as such very logical for a riddle to use the camel image. And from the coastal regions, the coconut is the most common tree. In fact, there are so many riddles from the coast that talk about the coconut. The one above gives us a concrete summary of the uses it is put to. The stem goes for firewood and building poles. Its branches are used for firewood or roofing 'Makuti'. The fibrous cover to the nut can be used as fuel or to make mattresses. The hard shell is shaped into ladles and today, bangles and hair clips. The nut is used for making cooking juice – copra or just eaten directly while the juice is drunk. Paralleling the coconut to the cow is thus a very effective comparison. The cow's carcass is food; its hooves, bones and horns can be carved into artifacts; the skin goes for leather; and the tail is used for making fly-whisks while the droppings are manure.[13]

It is not out of the way then to conclude that riddles acquaint the young mind of the riddler with compact knowledge of the environment and also the socio-cultural activities of the people. When we consider the stock of riddles from any given community, we are very likely to state their diet, religion, customs, economic activities and the climate, with reasonable accuracy.

Taking a more minute outlook, riddles act as a means of defining objects. As a child develops, the mind gains maturity in dealing with many things at a time. But during early childhood, especially years two to seven, the mind can only handle one thing at a time. The child can only think in one dimension. Riddles act as a tool for making the child comprehend his environment. They fragment the objects by referring to their various characteristics in different riddles. Later when the child is mature, he can synthesise all these and construct a full picture of the concept. For example, the following riddles define an egg.

Challenge: *Oda ma onge dhoot.*
              My house has no door
Response: *Tong'.*
              An egg.

LUO

Challenge: *Sanduku motamo wasunge yawo.*
              A box that even the whiteman can't open.

22

| Response: | *Tong'*. |
| | An egg. |

LUO

Challenge:	*Gima iye ring'o to oko chogo.*
	A thing that is meat inside and bone outside.
Response:	*Tong'*.
	An egg.

LUO

The egg is described here as a doorless container. It has neither an inlet nor an outlet. The only access to its contents is by breaking the shell. Using it is therefore similar to destroying the shell.

The outer shell is depicted as a bone, implying hardness and brittleness. The inside is 'meat', implying softness and edibility. Well, the egg is important to man in very many ways. The two obvious ones are as food and when it hatches into a chick. But from modern experience, the list can be lengthened, to include its uses as an emetic, and for beauticians, as shampoo. Through the riddles, the egg has been fully defined in terms of its physical characteristics and uses.

But one may wonder why it is only the egg that is said to have no door. What about oranges, mangoes, pears or coconuts? A close look reveals that the fruits have a kind of opening where they were attached to the twigs or roots. Perhaps it is only artificial articles like rubber balls, plastic toys or such manufactured items that may rival the egg. But the egg is organic while they are not and hence the comparison is illogical.

As much as we appreciate the effectiveness of riddles in depicting the environment, we note that there are riddles common to many communities. Some are exactly the same but others differ. It is this difference that needs our attention in analysing the geographical variations. Look at the following versions of the same epigram from different Kenyan communities.

| Challenge: | A person has sweet potato vines, and a leopard and a goat. He would like to cross a pond. How would he cross? |
| Response: | He would take the potato vines and the leopard first. Then he would return and pick the goat.[19] |

GIKUYU

| Challenge: | A man who had a lion, a goat and some grass wanted to cross a river. His boat could only carry one thing at a time. He could neither leave the lion with the goat nor the goat with the grass. How did he cross? |

Response: He first took the goat. Then he came back and took the lion. On reaching the other side, he left the lion and came back with the goat. He left the goat on the first side and took the grass. Finally, he came back for the goat.[20]

MIJIKENDA

Challenge: There was a man travelling with his wife and two friends. He also had a tame leopard and a goat. He had to cross a river in a boat which could only carry three things at a time. He was a very jealous husband and his leopard really liked goat. How did he get everybody across the river?

Response: He first took his wife and goat. Then he came back for his two friends. Leaving the friends on the other side, he picked the wife and returned with her for the leopard.[21]

SOMALI

First of all, the three riddles have some features in common. In each there is a predator, a goat and some barrier of water to be crossed. The presence of the goat in all the riddles is very significant. It tells us that this animal is common in those regions of Kenya. It is a hardy animal that can survive in the rather cold wet climate of Kikuyuland as well as the warm humid climate of Coastal Province and also the rather arid conditions of Somaliland.

These similarities notwithstanding, there are noticeable differences. In the Gikuyu and Mijikenda riddles, there is reference to potato vines and grass respectively. This shows that the weather can sustain some vegetation in the two places. The arid Somali surrounding cannot do that except for the scanty pasture for the animals. Secondly, the Mijikenda riddle has a lion while the other two have a leopard. We remember that lions are more common in the coastal region where we have the Tsavo National Park. Thirdly, there is no boat in the Gikuyu riddle and the barrier to be crossed is a pond. Gikuyuland is generally hilly hence no incidence of serious flooding. In most places we get some streams that can be waded at points. Meanwhile, the coast is the flood plain for rivers. The Indian Ocean's presence also shows that boats are a common feature there. What about the Somali case? The seasonal rivers in the regions occasionally flood and have to be crossed by some water vessel. It is probable that the vehicle referred to as a boat may be some contraption like a raft other than a conventional boat.

These riddles demonstrate the diversity in environment that riddles portray.

Pedagogy

J. Blacking in *The Social Value of the Venda Riddles* remarks that:

> If the mechanical acquisition of knowledge is of any value in the training of the mind, then it may be said that the learning of the riddle is important educationally.[22]

The phrase "mechanical acquisition of knowledge" proposes that knowledge of riddles, and the environmental figures they contain, comes from practice and experience. If we take riddles as fixed forms that are memorised and transmitted the same way from person to person, from generation to generation, then the learning of riddles as a consequence is the training of memory. But we earlier saw that the epigrammatic riddles do not rely wholly on memory but require wit. This is explored further below under mathematics and logic.

Since the mind (brain) is the centre of all intellectual processes, anything that effects it is important educationally. We can confidently say that riddles are a basic facility in education. This demands that we examine riddles not only in terms of traditional roles such as entertainment, but also their relevance to classroom education today.

The theory of education sees learning and teaching as a process of active interaction between the learner and the teacher. Communication is paramount to the success of any teaching and learning.

Riddles can superbly aid in this communication as a way of introducing, developing or even concluding a lesson in a given subject area. Below are examples of how riddles are academic.

Language Training

One obvious thing is the abundance of figures of speech especially metaphors, in riddles. The learning of metaphors leads the youth in his ability to use language with shades of meaning and hence enrich his communication skills.

As a system of human communication, language relies on a combination of sounds to relay meaning. By tradition, people associate certain words to signify certain specific objects or ideas. In some cases, the sounds in riddles may not form anything that may be called a meaningful word. These are the riddles we called phonologues, where the sound imitates the appearance, behaviour or use of the object by a sound. Most phonologues play on alliteration and thus assist the youth in pronunciation.

Furthermore, there are riddles that are more subtle, in the form of **puns** and **witticisms**. Punning refers to the ability to twist words. 'Lie' can mean, for example, being in a horizontal position or 'saying untruths'. One can play around with such words to create

25

confusion and humour. Ability to pun is an indication of mastery of language. Look at the following examples:

Challenge: The biggest bar in the world

UNDIFFERENTIATED

Anybody hearing this riddle for the first time starts remembering all places he knows selling alcohol to figure out the biggest of them all. He may even attempt looking through the Guiness Book of Records for this bar. If not, he may consult a dictionary or encyclopaedia. But his greatest surprise is when he finally hears that the answer to that riddle is 'Zanzibar'.

Challenge: What did the phone say to the other?

Response: You are too young to be engaged.

UNDIFFERENTIATED

Here the pun is on the word 'engaged'. It can mean "occupied", "busy" or "attached for marriage". The emphasis is on the last in that the phone is inanimate and cannot be married, yet we always hear people talking of phones being 'engaged'!

Witticisms are those riddles that actually trick the respondents. A witticism will require the respondent to stop and think the sense in what appears nonsensical. Have a go at this one.

Challenge: How many wheels does a car have?

UNDIFFERENTIATED

Like everyone else, perhaps you are sure that a car has only four wheels – the ones on which it moves. The riddle says it has 'Five!' How? Is the fifth the spare wheel? No. It is the steering wheel. How witty the riddle is!

Probably you have heard the story of the watchman who lost his job when he narrated to his employer a dream he had had during the night. Why was he instantly sacked? Consider this riddle with that information in mind.

Challenge: A question you cannot answer 'Yes!'

Response: 'Are you asleep?'

UNDIFFERENTIATED

Mathematics and Logic

Many riddles deal with numbers and indirectly teach the youth counting and general number work. Looking at the riddles on the human body, we come across a number of them that specify the number of eyes, ears, limbs, buttocks, breasts e.t.c. that the body has. We will take three examples:

26

Challenge:	Thirty-two seated, one lady dancing.
Response:	Teeth and the tongue.

UNDIFFERENTIATED

Challenge:	*Afar fallarood god wadagale.*
	Four arrows meet in a hole simultaneously.
Response:	*Geela marka lailsayo.*
	Milk entering a gourd during milking.

SOMALI

Challenge:	*Nyatiende ariyo mobet e wi nyatiende ang' wen karito nyatiende aboro.*
	The two-legged sitting on the four-legged waiting for the eight-legged.
Response:	*Winyo mobet e wi dhiang' karito okwodo.*
	A bird on a cow waiting for a tick.

LUO

At a glance we learn that the human being has thirty-two teeth in total, the camel's teats are four, the bird's legs two, the cow's four and the tick's eight. This kind of knowledge is a good base for further development in mathematics.

Mathematics and logic always go hand in hand. There are a number of riddles that test logic. Many such riddles are epigrams, in fact, mainly sleuths. For instance:

Challenge:	There were two mothers and two daughters. They went to visit someone and were given three chairs. All of them sat on the chairs without sharing or anyone carrying the other. How was this possible?[23]

UNDIFFERENTIATED

Without employing logic, there appears to be four people in the riddle. What does the response say?

Response:	One was a grandmother and her daughter who had a daughter also.

Logic argues it very well that the grandmother to the grandchild was a mother to the mother of the child. Hence two mothers and two daughters.

Going further, we encounter more riddles which convey even more advanced mathematical ideas of dimensions, shapes, sizes, space and time. Like these two:

Challenge:	*Maitũ ni mũkuhĩ baba ni mũraihu na mari ciana ikũmi na igĩrĩ.*
	My mother is short, father is tall and they have twelve children.

27

Response: *Thaa.*
              The watch or clock.

GIKUYU

This riddle says many things not only about the symmetry of the watch but also on people. The watch is a unitary system, like a family. The twelve hourly divisions are imagerised as children. The points are visited regularly by the hour and minute hands. The short hour hand is the mother while the long minute hand is the father. Why? Generally, females are shorter than males. Also, the traditional image of a father is that of a roamer, a being rarely at home and that of the mother as the more sedentary parent. Of course the minute hand is more mobile and the hour hand more stationary. For every one hour, the minute hand moves twelve steps while the hour hand only moves one similar step. So it is the hour hand that is in closer and longer contact with the stations like the mother is traditionally the parent more intimate with the children. But they are complementary in bringing up the family just like the hour and minute hands are in indicating time. So this riddle uses mathematical comparisons to state a fact of social life.

Challenge:.   My grandfather walks on four in the morning, two at midday and
              three in the evening.
Response: A person crawls in infancy, walks in youth and uses a walking-
              stick in old age.

UNDIFFERENTIATED

Focus here is on the posture and movement versus time and age. But from that we can infer important ideas of development and growth. Essentially, a person's experiences in childhood and adulthood determines what he becomes in old age. The average of these experiences paints the picture of the final personality. The equation can be expressed this way:

$$\frac{4(\text{crawling}) + 2(\text{walking})}{2(\text{average})} = 3(\text{walking - stick})$$

Further still, taking the nuclear family, we can see that in infancy the baby is cared for by every member of the family unit: father, mother, brother, and sister (4). The adult relies on himself and the spouse (2). In old age one relies on himself, the spouse and the offsprings (3). The offspring is the third leg equated with the walking-stick. The movement is from the quadrangular to the biangular to the triangular.

Geometrically, a four-sided figure is called a plane, and a three-sided one a space but the two-sided is not a figure. For stability, three legs is central. Two legs is a return to precariousness and instability. A four-legged object with one or two legs disproportionate

28

in length will always rest on the three legs. The fourth leg is therefore an addition that can be done without.

Using this model, it is rational to state that as a person grows, he sheds off dependence rapidly ending in an equilibrium. The physiological and psychological experiences undergone stabilise the person. The 4-2-3 model then signifies them: infant dependence – mature independence - aged consolidation. Again here, a riddle that appears simple actually carries a lot of implications.

Science

In this third section we look at how riddles can be used as springboards for teaching science. Let us consider Biology and Physics.

Biology is probably the field with the largest number of references in Kenyan riddles. There are riddles on human anatomy, reproduction, organs, plants, insects, e.t.c. Our example here is on the heart:

Challenge: My watch works every minute.
Response: The heart.

UNDIFFERENTIATED

Basically the comparison here is of the ticking of the watch with the thumping of the heart. The heart is a central organ of the body which pumps, distributes and recycles blood through the arteries, veins and capillaries. It resembles the watch which shows time through the hour, minute and second hands. There is also the quarterly division of both that can be tabulated as follows:

Watch	Heart
12.00 to 3.00 o'clock	Left Atrium
3.00 to 6.00 o'clock	Left Ventricle
6.00 to 9.00 o'clock	Right Ventricle
9.00 to 12.00 o'clock	Right Atrium

The importance of the heart is contained in the riddle as it states that the heart works every minute. When it stops working, life ceases unless sustained by very advanced scientific techniques.

Another appropriate example on organic functions is:

Challenge: A European peeping through the window.
Response: Mucus.

UNDIFFERENTIATED

29

The nose acts as the window into the body. It is an inlet for fresh air and outlet for deoxygenated air just like the window also circulates the air from inside and outside the house. From this riddle, the whole Biology lesson can be built on the respiratory process.

A physics teacher introducing the topic 'work' may riddle:

Challenge: *Ngwate kisithe natuithi*.
Catch my tail and let us go.

Response: *Iembe*.
A jembe (hoe).

KAMBA

The lesson can then be developed as follows: When digging, energy from the digger is passed on to the ground through the jembe. The amount of digging done is the area of the place covered. In which case, work done is equivalent to the force applied multiplied by the distance covered. Hence in physics:

Work (w) = Force (F) x Distance (d)

The few examples illustrate that indeed riddles are useful tools in conveying technical information.

Cultural Norms

Culture is simply a way of life. A people's culture embodies their language, religion, beliefs, customs, practices, economic activities, manner of dressing, forms of entertainment and eating habits. Each culture holds certain things as desirable and have standards to be adhered to. Anybody who does contrary to the standards is scorned. These standards are what are called norms. They vary with sex, age and social positions. Indeed they differ from community to community. Like the religious norms, general cultural norms are also expressed in terms of 'don'ts'. For instance, a child is not expected to exchange words with his parents however offended he is.

Riddles reflect to us the physical, social and cultural environment of a people. They do this through images. Most of these images are personifications i.e. things are talked of as if they were human sons, daughters, fathers, mothers e.t.c. Ordinarily, people personify objects they are closely attached to like cars, pets, furniture and musical instruments. Thus we get dogs called Dick, Bob or Tom.

The personification in riddles is not a chance occurrence. Why are some things referred to as feminine and others masculine, some children others adults? A natural pattern can be established by analysing the riddles themselves.

Challenge: I have a wife. Everybody she bears has a beard.

30

Response:	The maize plant.

Challenge: *Mamangu kazalia mwituni.*
My mother has given birth in the bush.

Response: *Nanasi.*
The pineapple.

Challenge: *Nyara ma kanywol to pielo nyithindo e lo.*
My daughter who gives birth by excreting on the ground.

Response: *Budho.*
The pumpkin.

All the above riddles talk about reproduction. Note that all the reproducing objects are female – "my mother" and "my daughter". Though we know that both male and female unite to realise reproduction, the mechanism centrally rests on the female.

In many traditions, a barren woman is considered incomplete. Regardless of her prettiness, hospitality and other virtues, a woman's crowning glory rests on fertility. By portraying the female as the main factor in reproduction, the riddles are simply restating the cultural expectation.

The woman's central role is not only biological, it is also social. She is the organiser of the home, co-ordinating matters on diet, hygiene, children's welfare and essentially everything that makes a home. This fact is contained in the riddles below:

Challenge: *Nikanini lakini mwenyu ndakasinda kuua.*
A small married woman who cooks better than your mother.

Response: *Nzuki.*
The honey bee.

Challenge: *Nina msichana mzuri lakini hagusiki.*
I have a very good girl but she is untouchable.

Response: *Moto.*
Fire.

Challenge: *Fatuma mchafu.*
The dirty Fatuma.

31

Response: *Kifagio.*
              The broom.

Challenge: *Mama nieleke.*
              Mother carry me.
Response: *Kitanda.*
              The bed.

Challenge: *Nyara ma wuok ka odenyo to duogo ka oyien' g.*
              My daughter who leaves hungry but returns full.
Response: *Mbiru.*
              The waterpot.

Challenge: My daughter has one eye on the head.
Response: The needle.

Challenge: *Nyara ma tiyo ma onge yweyo.*
              My daughter who works tirelessly.
Response: *Chuny.*
              The heart.

In traditional life, it is the woman who cooks, carries children, collects water, sews, sweeps and works tirelessly around the home. She never seems to have time to rest. Her typical day revolves around collecting firewood, fetching water, preparing food, gardening, looking after the children and finally jumping into bed where the husband is waiting. In this respect, she really resembles the heart that keeps pumping to keep man alive during the day and night. Considering the waterpot riddle, an interesting parallel is noticed. That space in the waterpot for water is like the woman's womb. Water is a symbol of life; the womb carries life. It would be most absurd to talk of the articles as male. In future we may, considering the rapid change in gender relations which is leading to the sharing of domestic chores.

Another characteristic considered seriously of the female person is beauty. The hierarchy of a woman's qualities ranks physical attractiveness very high. It is the visible indicator of her worth although not always is a pretty woman virtuous. Some riddles construct to us what is expected from a woman as observed from experience, as concerns physical appearance.

a. Challenge: *Fatuma mchafu.*
   The dirty Fatuma.
   Response: *Kifagio.*
   The broom.

SWAHILI

b. Challenge: *Agnes maridadi.*
   The colourful Agnes.
   Response: *Kinyonga.*
   The chameleon.

SWAHILI

Fatuma and Agnes are female names. *"Fatuma mchafu"* implies that Fatuma should not be dirty. In real life, a dirty girl is likely to be scolded more than an equally dirty boy. Females are expected to be clean. Likewise, they are keener and more colourful in dressing; they will always try to match colours and choose appropriate dressing for occasions. When a male adopts this kind of sensitivity in dressing he becomes a fop and very conspicuous. And there is a riddle for him.

c. Challenge: A gentleman who changes clothes whenever he goes.
   Response: The chameleon.

UNDIFFERENTIATED

The tone of riddle (b) is that of admiration while that of riddle (c) is flat and disgusted.

d. Challenge: *Nyara ma lando.*
   My brown (light-skinned) daughter.
   Response: *Mbiru.*
   The waterpot.

LUO

e. Challenge: *Nyara ma iye odwer.*
   My thin-waisted daughter.
   Response: *Pino.*
   The wasp.

LUO

The Luo are generally dark coloured; in fact they are distinctly darker than the Bantu groups. For them the light skin colour is rare and therefore more attractive. That is why the brown waterpot is valued and admired more than the black cooking pot.

Coming to the wasp riddle, it is common knowledge that body shape also contributes to beauty. Incidentally, current beauty contests require the contestants to submit the

33

measurements of their busts, loins and waist. The ideal shape is that which is thinnest at the waist and broadest at the hips. It is idiomatically called the figure 8 or the coca-cola bottle. One may even suspect that the contest borrowed its standards from the wasp.

f.   Challenge: Thirty two seated, one lady dancing.
      Response: The teeth and the tongue.

UNDIFFERENTIATED

g.   Challenge: *Adundo miel to ifuke.*
                    Adundo dances as she is rewarded.
      Response: *Mach.*
                    The fire.

LUO

Dancing is a way of displaying the bodily form. It is significant that the famous music groups have many male vocalists and instrumentalists, but female dancers. Riddle (f) says that one lady among gentlemen creates a decorative difference. She is dancing, entertaining, teasing spectators, deductively men. And in riddle (g) she is rewarded for her dancing. The practice of rewarding musicians and dancers is common in Luoland. They are showered with coins and portable gifts on the spot as appreciation of their artistry.

h.   Challenge: *Grace anapendwa na kila mtu.*
                    Grace is liked by everybody.
      Response: *Pesa.*
                    Money.

SWAHILI

A girl who is beautiful, Grace in this case, attracts all and sundry. In today's world, the one thing that everyone seems to like is money. Money is looked for with the same zeal as beauty.

While it is true that sex is not always arbitrary in riddles, there are cases where sex is not the most important aspect. In such cases, the image in the riddle can be female or male without changing the meaning or implication. At times, the riddles have neutral references e.g.:

  Challenge: *Wavulana wangu wanakimbizana lakini hawapatani.*
                    My sons are chasing one another but they never catch up.
  Response: *Magurudumu ya motokaa.*
                    The wheels of a car.

SWAHILI

The same riddle can be presented as:

34

Challenge: *Watoto wangu wanakimbizana lakini hawapatani.*
                 My children are chasing one another but they never catch up.
Response: *Magurudumu ya motokaa.*
                 The wheels of a car.

SWAHILI

The important aspect here is not the sex but the energy of play.

Finally, norms are conveyed even in the performance of riddles. When the respondents fail to get the answer, the challenger is given a prize. Among the Luo, the prize is a 'bride' or 'groom' depending on the challenger's sex. The challenger has the option to accept or reject the prize. He will always reject girls known to be careless, lazy, rude and clumsy in managing domestic duties. The female challenger will reject those boys known to be lazy, greedy and weak. Through this, riddling becomes a means of discouraging character traits that are undesirable in married life.

From the coastal groups, the prize is a town and is never rejected. This is because originally, the Arab occupants of the area always gave the town Mecca, the headquarters of Islam as the prize. Nobody would dare reject such a prestigious gift. In a way, getting the prize in the riddle kept the ambition in the children of going on the highly respected 'Hajj' (pilgrimage).

A second point in the riddling is its rotational nature. Everyone is expected to participate as a challenger and/or respondent. The principle here is that of give and take. It develops confidence among peers and encourages social interaction.

Social Commentary and Entertainment

As much as riddles are created from the pnysical environment, they also comment about human affairs. This is an activity that all forms of literature do. By considering the riddles, it will be appreciated that riddles are no exception. In this section, we deal particularly with how riddles convey humour and satire as they comment on different issues.

Humour and satire are literary aspects that are inseparable from the entertainment function of literature. The word entertainment is simple yet so difficult. People always talk about entertainment to mean amusement through activities like listening to music, watching films and spectating at games. Entertainment is thus the derivation of pleasure. In literature, the idea should be considered to encompass active participation in the creation and consumption of the work of art. Especially with oral literature, the performer is as much entertained by his art as the audience. So when talking of entertainment in riddles, there is no restriction to passive derivation of pleasure by an audience. Rather, it includes the following facts:

First, the atmosphere of entertainment must be free and fairly informal. There is a mutual understanding among all those present and none assumes superiority over the others. Secondly, due to this freedom, there is no coercion. One is present at the place because of his personal choice and contributes willingly to the activity going on. Thirdly, there must be activity and interaction between those present. The spectators at a football match are as much entertained by the match as they entertain themselves. That is why there is so much fun even before the match starts. It can therefore be said that the sheer presence at a stadium for a match is a form of entertainment. In the end, the total effect of all these aspects of entertainment is the refreshment of all the participants.

The social commentary and the humourous aspects are intertwined in riddles. We see that a riddle that on the surface invokes laughter in us, if analysed closely, may end up making a serious statement about our behaviour. Consider the following riddles on food and eating.

a. Challenge: *Mzee kipara ameingia.*
   The bald-headed old man has entered.
   Response: *Ugali.*
   Ugali (stiff porridge).

   SWAHILI

b. Challenge: *Polo omor ji ringo dwaro arunge.*
   There is thunder people rush for clubs.
   Response: *Chiemo ochiek ji dhi e mesa.*
   Food is ready people go to the table.

   LUO

c. Challenge: *Abolo tong' nyaka loka cha.*
   I have thrown the spear yonder.
   Response: *Amuonyo kuon nyaka e ich.*
   I swallowed ugali into the stomach.

   LUO

d. Challenge: *Kunywa supu tupa nyama.*
   Drink the soup, discard the meat.
   Response: *Miwa.*
   Sugarcane.

   SWAHILI

The humour in these riddles is mainly conveyed through **hyperbole** – the use of exaggeration usually to cause amusement and criticise. In the first riddle, bald is presented as a physical deformity and made to appear funny when it is called 'ugali'. The second

36

depicts the arrival of food as an invasion and it is as if people are to defend themselves with clubs. The imagery here lies in the fact that in eating, the Luo use their bare hands using the fingers and the palm to chunk off and shape the boluses of ugali. The fingers, in this process, actually form club-like fists. In this battle of eating, the eater usually gets defeated when his stomach cannot hold any more. And riddle (d) gives us a paradox: meat is thrown away in preference for soup. Most people would clear the meat without as much as looking at the soup. But in the case of sugarcane, solid residue must be discarded and the liquid juice (soup) swallowed. Now let's take a look at the following:

Challenge: *Piny rach ka koth ochwe.*
The earth is ugly after rains.
Response: *Jawuoro rach ka taya otho.*
The glutton is dangerous in darkness.

LUO

Here greed is denounced. We cannot help imagining the probable acts of the glutton in darkness: he could be salivating uncontrollably, switching plates, removing food from others' plates or swallowing huge chunks of food. In a sense he is as nauseating as the mud after rains. If the lamp is lit before he is through with his acts, he would be most embarrassed.

Well, once food has been eaten, it is digested and the nutrients taken in by the body tissue while the waste is expelled. Riddles have something on the waste products.

a. Challenge: *Ndatema mūti ndatiga ūgītoga.*
I cut a tree and left it steaming.
Response: *Mai.*
Excrement.

GIKUYU

b. Challenge: *Chogo gi kado.*
Bone and soup.
Response: *Chieth gi lach.*
Excrement and urine.

LUO

c. Challenge: *Eshikulu namuliango.*
A hill on the verandah.
Response: *Amafwi.*
Excrement.

LUHYIA

37

d. Challenge: *Nyara ma ka akalo to nyaka abolne simon.*
                Whenever I pass near my daughter, I must drop her a fifty cent coin.
    Response: *Chieth.*
                Excrement.

LUO

e. Challenge: A European peeping through the window.
    Response: Mucus.

UNDIFFERENTIATED

In African societies, sex and excretion are taboo and are referred to in euphemes since direct reference sounds crude. For instance, the riddles call bog a tree, a bone, a hill and a daughter. We get embarrassed in talking about these things. Yet they are a part of us that we cannot do away with. By euphemising them, riddles compromise us with their inevitability and make us accept them. The riddles also train us to call them politely, in a socially acceptable language.

Riddle (d) makes a serious comment on our behaviour. The refuse is personified as "my daughter" and hence elevated in value. Human beings who "give birth" to it (notice the similarity between giving birth and disembowelling) despise it by spitting whenever it is seen. Ironically however, spitting at it means acknowledging its presence without fail and rewarding it. The riddle is then laughing at man's contradictory attitude towards something in his nature.

Mucus is referred to as a European, a stranger, an intruder. Why is he peeping? To see the riches he can exploit in Africa? Suppose the mucus is not removed from the body and it remains bottled in there? The body would be unhealthy. Its removal purifies the body. Likewise the European colonist needed to be ejected from Africa for political health.

How did the European establish his rule in Africa? He built offices and institutions from where he co-ordinated his activities. A riddle summarises this idea so excellently:

Challenge: *Nyar msungu ni e ofis.*
            The white lady is in the office.
Response: *Mneme.*
            The jigger.

LUO

In a nutshell, riddles cannot be disregarded as vehicles of social comments. The performance itself is a process of interaction which creates a lot of entertainment also.

38

Record of Change

Literature, being based on a given time in history, place and society, has a setting. All literature is a product of a given social setting. They give a glimpse of the influences bearing upon the people. It can be stated confidently that literature is a sisterwing to history. The only difference is that history gives the facts as they are while literature seeks to interpret the facts using language in an artistic manner and presenting the same reality in fiction. As a genre of oral literature, riddles participate in this recording of change as it comes. There are specific riddles that can be said to have been composed at a particular time.

Things that are quite captivating get preference in attention. It will be noted that riddles are quite selective in recording these changes. Technological inventions like vehicles lend themselves easily to the attention of riddles. We remember that the first train to pass through Kenya did so not more than a century ago. There is a historical record of how this train was attacked by the Maasai and the other plains' people using spears in the belief that it was a snake. Here are some riddles referring to the train.

a. Challenge: *Gacha ringo e pap.*
   My train is running in the field.
   Response: *Ogonglo.*
   The centipede.

LUO

b. Challenge: *Thuol mayweyo iro.*
   The snake that exhales smoke.
   Response: *Gare.*
   The train.

LUO

c. Challenge: *Ndakinya ceceni ndoigirwo mbu.*
   On arrival at the station, I was shouted at.
   Response: *Ngari ya mwaki.*
   A train.

GIKUYU

Riddle (a) compares a centipede to a train. The jointed parts of the insect correspond to the coaches of the train and the legs to the wheels. Two ideas come out through riddle (b). First, the shape of the train is like that of the snake. Second, the train is said to breathe. Its smoky breath is paralleled with the snake's poisonous spittle. Remember that smoke is also a pollutant. Meanwhile, the Gikuyu riddle gives us another characteristic of trains;

their hooting as they arrive at or leave a station. Only a person who is out of his mind can see these riddles existing before the advent of the train.

Research on riddles shows that even the most recent innovations are recorded. Consider this Nairobi-based riddle:

Challenge: There was a dwarf working at the Kenyatta Conference Centre. He was always the first to arrive and the last to leave. He worked on the 28th floor but never used the lift when going up. He only used the lift when coming down. Why?

Response: He could never reach the top floor button (28th) when going up but could easily get to the ground floor button when coming down.

UNDIFFERENTIATED.

The Kenyatta Conference Centre was built in Post-Independence Kenya. And the installation of lifts is a very recent development. In fact, lifts are only known to exist in major Kenyan towns. Yet this riddle has recorded that development so aptly. This proves beyond doubt how effective riddles are in taking changes into account.

Saying that riddles record change is another way of stating that the stock of riddles develops both now and in history. At any given time, there are a number of riddles that talk about the same concept. The total of all riddles at a specific time in history gives us what may be considered a horizontal axis. To exemplify, look at these riddles existing on the mushroom:

Challenge: *Ndatsia wa kuka nendia ingokho yeshilenje shilala.*
              I went to my grandfather's and ate a one-legged chicken.

Response: *Olwoba.*
              The mushroom.

LUHYIA

Challenge: *Mwarabu anasimama kwa mguu mmoja.*
              An Arab standing on one leg.

Response: *Uyoga.*
              The mushroom.

SWAHILI

Challenge: *Mabul.*
              Umbrella.

Response: *Obwolo.*
              The mushroom.

LUO

40

All these riddles exist now on the mushroom. But they give us different perspectives about the mushroom. The Luhyia riddle concerns its use as food, a delicacy comparable to chicken. The Swahili one, on the other hand, personifies it as an Arab, colour and the single-leggedness being the characteristic factor. Meanwhile, the Luo see it as an umbrella, shape of the head being the scale of comparison.

As years pass, more riddles are composed and added to those existing before. After a period of time – a month, year or number of years – an increasing number of riddles will be in existence. This gives the vertical axis in the development of riddles.

From this kind of dynamism, it is quite in order to speculate on potential riddles. We can very accurately expect riddles on the television, cameras, computers, bombs, e.t.c. if some do not already exist. A riddle like the following is very likely:

Challenge: A camera in my body.

Response: The eye.

While we anticipate this forward movement, the passage of time and technological changes render some riddles obsolete. If we refer to the riddles on the watch clock, it is noted that they are based on the type that possess the hour, minute and second hands. There is still an abundance of such watches and clocks, but they are being replaced fast by digitals which do not have the hands. If the digitals replace them completely, it would be ridiculous to use those riddles based on the earlier watch type to someone who may never have seen one.

As the genre grows, so it dies and sprouts anew. A seed must die to allow for the sprouting of new life.

NOTES

1. S.K. Akivaga and A. B. Odaga, *Oral Literature: A School Certificate Course*, Nairobi: Heinemann, 1982, p. 113.
2. J. Nandwa and A. Bukenya, *African Oral Literature for Schools*, Nairobi: Longman, 1983, p. 105.
3. Naomy Kipury, *Oral Literature of the Maasai*, Nairobi: Heinemann, 1983, p. 122-6.
4. The Abaluhyia riddles used in the text are written in the Kisa, Marama and Batsotso dialects.
5. The riddle was collected by Lydia Ndapatani.
6. I am indebted to Angela Simwenyi for this piece of information about the Somali procedure of riddling.
7. This riddling cycle also appears in *A Dictionary of Oral Literature* by Sunkuli and Miruka and published by Heinemann in 1990.
8. Roger D. Abrahams, *The Complex Relations of Simple Forms* included in Dan Ben Amos' (ed) *Folkrole Genres*, University of Texas Press, 1976.

9. The ideas of Gorges and Dundes are explored in Charles Scott's *On Defining the Riddle* in Dan Ben Amos' (ed) *Folkrole Genres*, University of Texas Press, 1976.

10. Scott, ibid.

11. Abrahams, ibid.

12. Ulli Beier. *African Poetry: An Anthology of Traditional African Poems*, London: Cambridge University Press, 1966, p. 23.

13. Ibid. p.64.

14. Ibid.

15. Ibid. p.68.

16. For the fuller story, see B. Onyango Ogutu and A. A. Roscoe's *Keep My Words*, Nairobi: East African Publishing House, 1974, p. 108.

17. This expression has been used by Austin Bukenya and Pio Zirimu in their unpublished manuscript "Oracy as a Tool for African Development".

18. I am indebted to Lydia Ndapatani for this interpretation.

19. Collected by Hezekiel Njoroge.

20. Collected by Lydia Ndapatani.

21. Collected by Angela Simwenyi.

22. J. Blacking, "The Social Value of the Venda Riddles" in *African Studies vol.20 No.1*, 1961, Witwatersrand University Press.

23. Collected by Sabina Okech.

PART TWO

PROVERBS

"Ciunagwo rũkomo, kimenyi akamenya ikiunwo."
"We speak by proverbs; he who is intelligent will understand."
Agikuyu Proverb.

What is a Proverb?

As a matter of definition, what we need to do first is to put proverbs in a social context. The society is the mother of culture. Any culture may be divided into two branches: the material and the social. Material culture refers to the physical products of human societies in response to the demands of the environment. This is where we get utensils, tools, furniture, attire, musical instruments, e.t.c. The social includes language, history, religion, philosophy, customs, etc. or compose the intangible elements of culture.

Proverbs belong to the realm of language. Language itself is part of the social culture. Basically, oral language is used to effect communication either nominally, artistically or in code. Oral Literature, to which proverbs belong is part of artistic communication. From this premise, we can see the placement of our subject area diagrammatically as presented below.

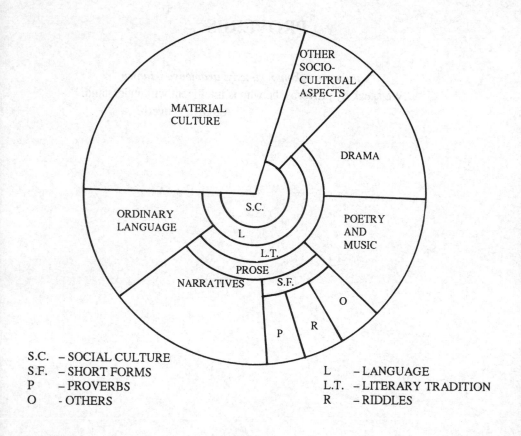

S.C. – SOCIAL CULTURE
S.F. – SHORT FORMS
P – PROVERBS
O - OTHERS

L – LANGUAGE
L.T. – LITERARY TRADITION
R – RIDDLES

Here we have classified the proverbs among the short forms. This is a term taken from Bukenya and Nandwa. Under 'Style and Structure', we shall delve into the issue of shortness and under the functions we shall see the relationship between proverbs and the other genres. Meanwhile we can note here that apart from the structural differences between narratives and poetry on the one hand with the short forms, the first two tend to be more direct in their meaning while the rest are less direct. Thus some people have called them the "gnomic forms", a derivation from the idea of a gnome: "a little man who lives under the ground and guards stores of gold".[22]

Briefly, we can state that the short forms consist of sayings and language games. The sayings are: proverbs, adages, apothegms or aphorisms, dicta, maxims, slogans, idioms and euphemes. The language games are: riddles, puns and tongue-twisters. There is inevitably a lot of overlap among the sayings. But all the same we can see a rough distinction into three groups: proverbs, aphorisms and adages; dicta, maxims and slogans; and finally idioms and euphemes.

In *The Complex Relations of Simple Forms*, Roger D. Abrahams does something somewhat similar to what we have attempted above. He classifies oral performances into the conversational, play, fictive and static genres. The conversational are those in which "one person directs his expression in an interpersonal fashion to a limited number of others as part of everyday discourse" e.g. slang, jargon, colloquialism e.t.c. In the play genres are those which are markedly divorced from everyday talk by their stylisation and some level of formality but which are still conducted in a relaxed reciprocal atmosphere with participants assuming specific roles. Here are included riddles, other word games and verbal contests. Coming to the fictive, we are now dealing with more removal of participants from real life and the assumption of explicit symbolic roles. Such genres tend to have a monologue type of performance and here is where we get narratives, for example. The last category, the static, contain those creations "where the performer expresses himself in a concrete form that remains after the moment of enactment", such works being paintings, sculpture and design.

Abrahams includes the proverbs among the conversational genres under the sub-genre which includes "superstitions, mnemonics, spells, curses, prayers, taunts and charms". He characterises them by their use of "formal conventions of the discourse of address, appeal and assault". Thus he comes up with a diagrammatic scale of relationships as follows:[1]

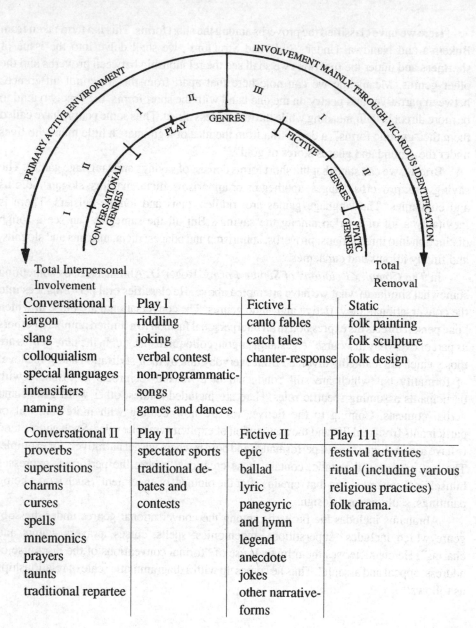

Total Interpersonal Involvement			Total Removal
Conversational I	Play I	Fictive I	Static
jargon	riddling	canto fables	folk painting
slang	joking	catch tales	folk sculpture
colloquialism	verbal contest	chanter-response	folk design
special languages	non-programmatic-		
intensifiers	songs		
naming	games and dances		

Conversational II	Play II	Fictive II	Play 111
proverbs	spectator sports	epic	festival activities
superstitions	traditional de-	ballad	ritual (including various
charms	bates and	lyric	religious practices)
curses	contests	panegyric	folk drama.
spells		and hymn	
mnemonics		legend	
prayers		anecdote	
taunts		jokes	
traditional repartee		other narrative-	
		forms	

The figure represents the range of interaction between performer and audience in the genres.

To come closer to our subject, let us take some of the published definitions of proverbs:

1. "A proverb is usually stated in the form of a maxim, epigram or aphorism" (Kipury, N. *Oral Literature of the Maasai*).

2. A proverb is a "short familiar sentence expressing a supposed truth or moral lesson; a byword; a saying that requires explanation (*Chambers 20th Century Dictionary*).

3. A proverb is a "short well known saying in popular language" (*Longman Dictionary of Contemporary English*).

4. A proverb "is a short saying of wisdom in general usage" (Akivaga, S. K. and Odaga, A. B. *Oral Literature: A School Certificate Course*).

5. A proverb is "a saying in more or less fixed form marked by shortness, sense and salt and distinguished by the popular acceptance of the truth tersely expressed in it" (Finnegan R. *Oral Literature in Africa*).

6. "A proverb is a terse, pithy statement containing folk wisdom" (Nandwa and Bukenya, *African Oral Literature for Schools*).

From these definitions we can sieve the integral ingredients of proverbs as:

a. Shortness, terseness or brevity.
b. Truth, wisdom, meaning or pithiness.
c. Obscurity, indirectness or gnomic nature.
d. Relative invariability of form.
e. Acceptance and usage by a community.

Taking the definition of a gnome as a base, we can derive a definition of a proverb as a brief statement full of hidden meaning, accepted and used by a community as an expression of truth or wisdom.

Noting that we are dealing with African proverbs in the main, we can turn our attention to some of the indigenous terms of the concept. It is interesting to note that many communities use the same word for a broad spectrum of ideas. This points to the integratedness of genres and the polysemy of language. The following table gives a brief summary of some of the terms and what they refer to.

Term	Meaning	Community	Country
Ngero (Pl. Ngeche)	Proverb, Allusion, Parable, Allegory, Riddle	Luo	Kenya
Thimo	Proverb	Kikuyu	Kenya
Ndung'eta-e-rashe	Proverb	Maasai	Kenya
Ndimo Ndimo	Proverb, Dark saying, Metaphorical wording	Kamba	Kenya
Mallol	Proverb, Allusion	Fulani	Nigeria
Tindol	Proverb, Popular moral story, Maxim	Fulani	Nigeria
Olugero	Proverb, Saying, Story, Parable	Baganda	Uganda

CLASSIFICATION OF PROVERBS

In academics, classification is a distinct branch of study, its aim being the differentiation of what otherwise belong together at some general level. From a community's point of view, there may be no rigid classification thus what scholars do when they classify is to try and organise corpus.

There are many actual and potential approaches to classification of proverbs as described below.

Alphabetical Classification

Using this approach, the corpus is arranged using the first letter/sound of the first word in the proverb and the subsequent letters/sounds in the order in which they occur in the alphabet. This is the system used by G. Barra in *1000 Kikuyu Proverbs* and S. S. Farsi in *Swahili Sayings I*.

The distinct advantage of this system is that it caters for all possible proverbs and is easy to execute. Its disadvantage may be that it puts together proverbs of diverse structures, styles and themes and hence does not differentiate at this level. Again, once the proverbs are translated into another language, the classes are put into disarray and others have to be developed.

48

Content or Thematic Classification

Under this, the proverbs are grouped according to the subject matter. It is one of the most commonly used systems. For example, Massek and Sidai use it in *Wisdom of the Maasai* while Naomy Kipury also uses it in *Oral Literature of the Maasai*. In the latter, proverbs are categorised under: Religion and paramountcy of God, Kinship relations, Caution, Warning against pretence, Cattle, Obvious aspects of life, Life in general, e.t.c. To illustrate how this system works, let us take a few examples of proverbs that might be classified as political.

1. *Jatelo ogongo gwaro.*
   The leader gets scratched by ogongo thorns.

LUO

This proverb may be used to talk about a leader who is facing difficulties in his task of leadership on behalf of his subjects. It depicts leadership as a sacrifice and not just a bed of roses.

The author collected this proverb during a campaign rally for councillorship in 1983 at Asembo-Bay. It was used by the defending councillor, Mr Amolo Kwesi. Being the incumbent, he was facing a barrage of attacks from the other contestants. In defence, he summarised the attacks as far-fetched and declared that in leadership it is impossible to satisfy everyone. Leadership, he added, is a very tough undertaking needing a very tactful person. He then narrated the difficulties he had weathered to achieve the pockets of progress during his tenure of office. Now that he had passed through, he was not regretting because he had paved the way for milk and honey to reach his constituents and hence the need to return him to office. The opponents used the same proverb to discredit him saying that if it were not for his failures, they would not be seeking to oust him. So they were now the thorns pricking him for his "inept" leadership.

2. *Meipurr oloing'oni too muruen are.*
   A bull cannot bellow in two settlements.

MAASAI

The idea of a leader bull in any herd is pervasive in Africa. It is the bull that commands the others. The proverb means that a person is only master over a given territory and should never trespass into others which also have their masters. Stretched further, this can be seen enshrined in the UN and OAU statutes that no country should interfere in the internal affairs of another sovereign country. The gist of the argument is that each country has its peculiarities and it is presumptuous for an outsider to imagine he can channel the destiny of the nation better than the insider.

49

An outsider may be overwhelmed by the responsibility and fail to deliver the goods in the final analysis and hence lose both sides. He may also get so engrossed in the new find that he gets undone in the old one. Likewise he may have underrated the prowess of the new territory which destroys him in defence against his infringements. So one should stick to his affairs and not pretend to be a jack of all trades since he is likely to end up a master of none.

The above analysis clarifies that the content approaches to classification can lead to an in-depth understanding and discussion of issues in the proverbs. The shortcoming that might be identified is that one proverb can be used multi-contextually, thus while it might mean one thing in one situation, it would mean a completely different thing in another situation.

For example, in *Wisdom of Maasai*, the following proverb appears under "Children".

Apaaya, mintudung' nkishu nkulie
Hallo, don't let one herd cross the path of another.

The explanation given is that a father should take care of his children just as he takes care of his cattle. For someone else who puts a high premium on parenthood and not children, the proverb could be classified under "Parents".

In the same text, we get the following proverbs all classified under "Parents".

1. *Meisudoo alowuaru olkujita.*
   A lion cannot hide in tall grass (i.e. a hypocrite will not go for long undetected).
2. *Metamakinoi emurt entakule.*
   The neck is not measured by the arm (i.e. all men are not granted things equally).
3. *Meoro enkaji nabo.*
   One house cannot be divided.

Still using the content approach, one may classify these proverbs not under "People" but under "Character" for 1, "Individual Differences" for 2, and "Solidarity" for 3. In other words, the word chosen to describe the class in this system is highly subjective.

Functional Classification

This approach operates from the theoretical framework that oral literature is not there for its own sake but for sociological purposes, principally that of educating. When a proverb is categorised under caution, warning, advising, e.t.c., the system used is that of functions i.e. what the proverb is meant to do.

Functional classification is very significant when we consider that oral literature is a product of culture. Through a people's oral literature, we can peep into their philosophy, beliefs, attitudes, morals, e.t.c. The proverb functions to propagate these aspects of the community. Like with content classification it could also be noted that functional classification cannot be rigid but has to operate along some kind of sociological slide rule as illustrated in the proverb below:

Jatelo ogongo gwaro.
The leader is scratched by ogongo thorns.

Depending on the context, the proverb can be used to:

1. Encourage a leader to keep on despite difficulties;
2. Advise a leader during his inauguration that leadership is a challenge and he/she should expect some rough times;
3. Criticise a leader who has been overwhelmed by pressures of leadership;
4. Summarise a situation where a leader has had to suffer for the sake of his/her followers.

But it should not be mistaken that this proverb can only be used in a political situation. Domestically, the same proverb can be used to awaken the first born son to his obligations to the younger siblings since in many African communities, certainly among the Luo, the elder children are expected to relieve their parents by taking care of the siblings once the parents are retired or aged.

Stylistic-Structural Classification

In this method, which the author proposes, the proverb is classified basing on the form of expression and the stylistic features it has. Out of this, we could have such classes as:
- Directives
- Epigrams
- Allusions

Directives

Most proverbs are statements that comment on situations, describe, sum up or are intended to convey some idea to targeted people. They point out the nature of the events and hence express the perceptions of the speaker about the event. In doing this, the proverbs are flavoured with authority and axiom as they are stated as objective truths seeking to guide human conduct. A few assorted examples are:

51

Emut olkurto enkop.
The worm can destroy a whole plain.

MAASAI

Ciatura ngũyũ iriaga ng'ũmo.
When there is shortage of figs, birds eat the fruits of the 'mũgumo'.

GIKUYU

Chako chon loyo dhi ajuoga.
Starting early is better than going to a medicineˑman.

LUO

Asiyefunzwa na mamaye hufunzwa na ulimwengu.
He who is not taught by the mother is taught by the world.

SWAHILI

There is often wisdom under a shabby cloak.

LATIN

Meibor ng' eno lukunya.
Wisdom is not always white-headed.

MAASAI

These proverbs impress by their statements of what are universal truths, principles that guide the actions and thoughts of a rational society. The first one exults the value of importunity as the basis of success. It corresponds to the Swahili *"Bandu! Bandu! Huisha gogo"* which means "Chip! Chip! Fell great oaks". In the second, the question of adaptation to changing circumstances is put so powerfully. It is a fact that adversity makes man very innovative and start to see value in what is ordinarily useless. Again the Swahili have a very apt saying to the same effect, viz: *"Simba akikosa nyama, hula nyasi"* i.e. when a lion misses meat, it eats grass". Coming to the third proverb, the position is that regrets can be forestalled or as the English say, "A stitch in time saves nine". The fourth is a reminder to the deviant that parental advice is after all not useless and failure to heed always lands a person in trouble. It is during time of trouble that he realises that he should have heeded the advice because the world has no sympathy. In other words, experience usually teaches people better than words. And the last two summarise a very potent truth; that there need not be anything physically conspicuous to mark a wiseman. Often it is a poor man, shabby in appearance that turns out to be sagacious.

52

Epigrams

These are the longer, usually amusing proverbs expressing some clever thought. Characteristically, epigrams draw analogies between phenomena. An epigram exists in at least two parts; both may be stated or one may be implied. This will become clearer in the following examples:

> Fear less, hope more; eat less, chew more; whine less, breathe more; talk less, say more; hate less, love more; and all good things will be yours.[2]

SWEDISH

> It is man who counts; I call upon gold, it answers not; I call upon cloth, it answers not; it is man who counts.[3]

GHANIAN

> *Maji yakijaa, hupwa; mpanda ngazi hushuka.*
> When the tide is high it ebbs; he who climbs the ladder comes down again.

SWAHILI

> *Mlilala handingwandingwa; mwemacho hambiwi tule.*
> A sleeping man doesn't feel the onset of hunger; a man who is awake is not told 'let's eat' (he knows when he's hungry).

SWAHILI

> Patience is power; with time and patience a mulberry leaf becomes silk.

CHINESE.

> From those I trust, God guard me; from those I mistrust, I will guard myself.

ITALIAN

As a literary form, the epigram compounds poetry, proverbs and riddles. The above examples could easily pass for short verses. Indeed *Longman Dictionary of Contemporary English* defines an epigram as "a short clever amusing poem or saying". The proverbialism occurs in the philosophy contained in the expressions. For example, if we consider the sixth proverb, the idea being hammered is that we should love all but trust none. The persona is more scared of the people he trusts than the adversaries. As the Swahili put it *"Kikulacho ki nguoni mwako"* i.e. "that which eats you is right inside your clothes".

And then there is the confounding relationship between proverbs and riddles. At some point it becomes difficult to distinguish the two. Ruth Finnegan in appreciating the overlap has this to say:

"Less common are the epigrams that occur among the Fulani as a form closely connected with both riddles and proverbs. They share the characteristics of grouping

53

together a number of phenomena which have some basic similarity or illustrate some general principle in the same way as riddles."[4]

She goes ahead to give two examples as follows:

1. Three exist where three are not;

    Commoners exist where there is no king, but a kingdom cannot exist where there are no commoners;

    Grass exists where there is nothing that eats grass, but what eats grass cannot exist where there is no grass;

    Water exists where there is nothing that drinks water, but what drinks water cannot exist where there is no water.

2. Three things are for three things except for three things;

    Sleep is like death but for breathing;

    Marriage is like slavery but for wifely respect;

    A guinea-fowl is like cloth but for being alive.[5]

FULANI

The above epigrams can be regarded as riddles with the first general statement as the challenge and the expanded explanation as the response. But considered a second time, they transcend the jocularity of riddles and state some proverbial ideas. For instance the analogy between sleep and death is a common one. The Luo actually say that sleep is the sister of death. The profundity elevates the expressions to the proverbial level.

How about a local Kenyan example?

Era ilmoruak ong'wan

There are four kinds of elders.

Panyoneishu doesn't prepare for the future; and therefore remains poor.

Tanya ee has a little property but is never increased.

Olchanuki also has little property but is fortunate to live a long life and see his grandsons circumcised.

Orrereta is wealthy and popular, but does not have as long a life as Olchanuki.

MAASAI

This is a summary of the socio-economic status of elders – people at the horizon of their lives and who do not hope to achieve more than they already have. The idea is that even though elders are often grouped together, they are distinct individuals. It is the metaphor of the tree in the woods.

From afar, the forest looks like a mass of wood but at close range, we begin to see single trees. The proverb is actually telling us that equality is relative. Not everyone receives the same treatment from nature or fate. Yet each does not desire to be another. As

54

the Greek sage, Socrates, once put it: if we were to exchange our woes, after a while, each one of us would ask for his/her own back.

Allusions

An allusion is an indirect reference to some familiar person, event, object or place. The familiarity of the concept makes the meaning of the work clear and actually gives it a context. Literature, proverbs included, is full of allusions as a stylistic feature.

By their very nature of being products of a people's history, proverbs abound in allusion, some historical (having base in events that actually happened), others fictional and yet others welleristic (ascribing the statement to an actual or fictional character).

Here are a few examples to illustrate the cases.

> *Ūkabi ni mūhūūnu mūtu.*
> The Maasai have had their fill of flour.
>
> GIKUYU

Recorded in G. Barra's *1000 Kikuyu Proverbs*, the history behind this proverb is that:

> The Kikuyu used to sell maize and millet flour to their neighbours, the Maasai. But if they happened to sell it a little too dear, the flour trade became the spark which kindled... many raids...
>
> *Ening' sirir king'a.*
> The clever child hears the secrets.
>
> MAASAI

The above proverb is about how Olonana (Lenana) came to be the Maasai spiritual and paramount chief ruling until 1911 as here explained by Massek and Sidai.

> When Mbatian, the great loibon felt death approaching, he told his eldest son to come to his hut early the next morning to receive his blessings and the secrets of the loibon. However, another son, Olonana, overheard the conversation and arrived in his father's hut even before the sun had arisen. The aging Mbatian thought it was Senteu before him in the dark and therefore gave Olonana the secrets of office meant for the elder brother.[7]
>
> *Itukurrua taake, anaa olotijina ilmong' le a Senteu, eata iltualan loo ilmurran le Loita.*
> You are as ashamed as the one who mingles with Senteu's oxen wearing the bells of Loita warriors
>
> MAASAI

The history behind this proverb is that:

> In the late 1890's, the Laikipiak Maasai near Nakuru decided to raid the Loita Maasai whose loibon was Senteu. As the Laikipiak were boasting of their certain victory, and the number of cattle they would return with, they were warned that the Loita were a formidable enemy. The Laikipiak paid no attention. However, they were soundly defeated by the Loita and only a few returned, bringing no cattle at all.[18]

These examples illustrate the historicity of proverbs hence making such proverbs factual allusions.

Of the fictional allusions, we could cite the following:

> 1. *Kinda ne omiyo opuk oyombo apuoyo.*
>   Persistence made the tortoise outrace the hare.

LUO

The proverb is derived from the story that there was once a race between Hare and Tortoise for a coveted prize. Confident of his superiority over the Tortoise, Hare raced but stopped on the way to browse. Meanwhile, Tortoise kept on and eventually won as Hare still enjoyed his food in the forest.

> 2. *Inotie enainotie le-enkipika the ming' ani.*
>   You have got what the son of Engipika got in the deserted kraal.

MAASAI

Here is the narrative base of the proverb:

> One day Ole Engipika was eating in the slaughter house when the place was attacked by an enemy. He managed to escape with his meat but without his weapons, hotly pursued by the enemy. After running some distance, he entered a deserted kraal where he proposed to hide. But he soon discovered he was not the only occupant, and a lion growled savagely at being disturbed. Thinking best to leave, he turned around and saw a serpent coiled around the gate post, the only exit. In the distance, he could see the enemy rapidly approaching. It is not related how Ole Engipika escaped from this dilemma.[9]

This story could very well be true. But it is more likely to be just a creation of the mind. It can be classified as a fictional allusion on the ground that Ole Engipika could be a stock name hence stand for anybody; the exact time and place of the event is not stated (presumably, it took place a long time ago); how the victim got out of the dilemma is not related; thus the important thing in the story is not the accuracy of facts but the simulation of a classic dilemma.

3. *Ndakūrama kīnganga nawe wanama kīngware.*
   I gave you the beauty of a guinea fowl and you gave me the beauty of a francolin.

GIKUYU

The proverb is based on the etiological tale that:

Once upon a time the guinea fowl, wanting to go to a dance, called upon the francolin to have its feathers dressed. The francolin, hoping to have the same favour returned by the guinea fowl, assented. But the latter, taking as an excuse of its laziness that the dance was about to begin, left the other bird in the lurch. This is why the guinea fowl has got much finer plumage than the francolin.

The last type of allusion is what we referred to as wellerism, where a proverb is introduced with a name tag purporting to name the person or character who said the proverb.

For example:

1. *Etejo opa olng' ojine, "Mme kamunyak oshi, keju maitagol".*
   The hyena once said, "I am not lucky, but I am always on the run".

MAASAI

2. Eneke the bird said that since men have learnt to shoot without missing, he has learnt to fly without perching.[10]

IBO (Nigeria)

PERFORMANCE AND STYLE OF PROVERBS

Proverbs, like the other genres of oral literature, are communicated by word of mouth. The word 'performance' is generally understood to mean the delivery or rendition of an item, usually to an audience. In the foregoing section, we saw the classification of proverbs among the conversational genres. Conversation is an interactive process where there is reciprocity between and among the speaker and his interlocutors. Using this as a parameter of argument, how accurately can we say that proverbs are performed?

It is the contention of the author that it is actually a misnomer to say that proverbs are performed in the same way as riddles, poems and narratives. The idea of performance nominally implies a demarcation between the performer and his audience. The performance is even guided by certain tacit regulations to which every participant subscribes. There is an orderly sequence of events and the context of performance is defined. For instance, narratives are traditionally told in the evening; there is one performer at a time;

there are formulas to introduce and conclude the performances; and finally there is a rotational order which is followed to accord each participant a chance to narrate a story.

With the proverbs, however, these aspects are absent. There is no demarcation of the speaker and the interlocutor – both are participating on the same plane; there are no regulations as to how and when to use a proverb; there are no formulas to cue the interlocutor that a proverb is on the way nor is there any expectation from either party that when one has used a proverb then the other must do the same.

The next thing we need to consider is the context of rendition of proverbs. Who uses proverbs, when, where, how and why? Are there restrictions as to the use of proverbs or some proverbs in particular? What kind of relationship pertains between the speaker and his hearer? Some of these questions have implicitly been answered in the foregoing paragraphs. However, there is much more to be said about proverbs and their rendition. One writer who gives us a headway in doing this is Peter Seitel who, in *Proverbs: A Social Use of Metaphor* discusses the structures underlying the use of proverbs under what he calls the interaction situation, proverb situation, context situation, correlation and strategy[11]. These aspects are explained later in this chapter when dealing with structure.

A question that can immediately be addressed here is that of who uses proverbs. It is not uncommon to find claims that it is elders who use proverbs. If this should be generally true, it is necessary not to take it as a rule. Rather, there should be a descriptive attitude towards the matter where a field worker does not go to the field with the predisposition that he will only get proverbs from elders but should be ready to record whatever is available without prejudice. From then on, it should be determined who uses proverbs predominantly and why that is so.

Elders may appear to use more proverbs in their speech because they are more adept at the language and have longer experience in life. Seitel explains this thus:

> Because it is necessary for the hearer of a proverb to know the features of the terms (so that he can understand the relationship and hence the metaphor), a child is told stories either along with proverbs or instead of them so that he can see the terms used in proverbs alone, in the environments which define their features. Alternatively, proverb use in general or the use of particular proverbs is delayed until a child is thought to have had sufficient social experience, to have observed the social environments which invest proverbs with their proper features.[12]

The point being raised then is that the youth learn proverbs as a matter of socialisation and hence develop usage abilities spontaneously without a mechanical barrier as to whether they can or not use them.

How about the sexes? Who, between men and women, use proverbs more regularly? On the surface, it would appear that men use proverbs with greater abandon. This may be so because men dominate public life and administration and therefore are more regularly in circumstances which demand speech-making. But in interpersonal conversation, women may be just as adept or even more so at using proverbs as or than the men.

ASPECTS OF STYLE

Structure

Peter Seitel gives us a very illuminating picture of the nature of proverbs, an analysis which has got a lot of bearing on this section of text. For studying proverbs, he suggests a look at what he terms as the interaction situation, proverb situation, context situation, correlation and strategy. What are these?

The interaction situation refers to the circumstances in which a proverb is spoken e.g. a meeting, formal ceremony, family discussion, e.t.c. This situation involves a speaker and the intended hearer who are related by aspects like sex, age, status, e.t.c. Thus the interaction situation can be illustrated as:

$$A : B$$

where A is the speaker, B the intended hearer and (:) the relationship between them e.g. father to son, elder to child, friends, e.t.c.

The use of a proverb by A then leads to the proverb situation. Let us imagine that a father is advising an errant son, one who heeds not anyone's advice. Such a father may tell the son that *"Asiyesikia la mkuu huvunjika guu"* (Swahili) i.e. "A disobedient child breaks his leg". The son has not broken a leg yet but the father is making an imaginary proposition that he could very soon. The metaphor constitutes a proverb situation which may be summarised as:

$$C * D$$

where C and D are concepts in the imaginary (metaphorical) situation and * represents the logical relationship between the two. This relationship may be explicitly stated or otherwise implied. In our example, it is explicit since we can talk of:

Asiyesikia la mkuu (C) *huvinjika* (*) *guu* (D),
A disobedient child (C) breaks (*) his leg (D).

The child is expected to decode the reference into a meaningful statement directed at him. This is what gives rise to the context situation. In our case, the father is telling the child, "You (as a disobedient child) will end up suffering". The claim being made is that the two concepts in the proverb situation translate into the two in the context situation. Thus the latter can be summarised as:

$$E * F$$

59

If the three situations are combined we come up with something like this:

A : B gives rise to C * D which means E * F.

In the above example, the father talks to the son. It is therefore a one to one context and the son is the subject of the proverb. Other situations pertain where the subject of the proverb is none of the conversationalists or where there is a one to many relationship. The possibility of various referents leads Seitel to talk of "correlation" i.e. what are the terms in the proverb to be matched with? Then we find that a single proverb can actually refer to so many things depending on who is saying it, to who and with what intention. Seitel gives an example with the Ibo proverb, "A toad does not run in the daytime unless something is after its life" which can be used in six or more different situations. But let us use the example that appears earlier in our text.

A Luo proverb says: *"Jatelo ema ogongo gwaro"* meaning, "It is the leader that gets pricked by the 'ogongo' thorns". When the author collected this proverb, it was used by a campaigner for the post of a councillor in Asembo-Bay, Siaya in 1983. The contestant was then facing criticism that he had not delivered enough to his constituents. But he retorted using the proverb to say that he had undergone a lot of hardship in laying the development strategies that had yielded what the opponents saw as the little he had achieved. Thus because he had now levelled off the barriers, it was ideal that he be re-elected to complete the task. He was equating himself with the leader referred to in the proverb and his problems were the thorns.

But his opponents used the very same proverb to discredit him. They said that he was a leader who had not lived up to their expectations and so they were the thorns pricking him out of office.

These are not the only two contexts within which the proverb can be used. It can also be used to:

1. Exhort a leader who is facing difficulties on behalf of his constituents and who is almost giving up;
2. Advise those aspiring for public offices that their prospective roles are difficult and they should prepare to face hardships;
3. Encourage pioneers in any project that success would only come from assiduity and resilience and that they should not expect things to be plain sailing;
4. Explain to the first born son in the African family that he would have to sacrifice a lot for the sake of his younger siblings, e.t.c.

Seitel also talks of "strategy" to mean the intent with which the proverb is used i.e. the proverb is a means of dealing with the situation named. Abrahams, another scholar, looks at proverbs and other genres as basically functioning strategically in the realm of "address, appeal and assault". In most cases, "the proverb sayer appeals, directly or by analogy, to an approved course of action which has been effective in the past. He does so to solve an immediate problem and to influence future attitudes or actions". Other such strategies are analysed under the social functions of proverbs.

This brief overview launches us into an examination of the physical anatomy of proverbs in terms of manner of expression and other literary devices.

In characterising proverbs, Nandwa and Bukenya have talked of their brevity, terseness, invariability and informality. Of structural importance to us here are the first three. Brevity has to do with the length. Proverbs are appreciably short statements, in comparison to the other genres. The terseness refers to the force with which proverbs put across their points. They do not bandy words but are very succinct. Meanwhile the invariability refers to the fixedness; proverbs are stated in more or less the same words always with very little lexical or syntactic change.

That is very true although there is some level of variation usually noticed and practised by speakers. This occurs in the form of abbreviations, syntactic and, in some cases, morphological changes. Abbreviation is where the speaker says only a part of the proverb and leaves the rest to be filled in by the listener. For syntactic rearrangement, let us take a Luo proverb for an example.

Jawuoth achiel rienga.
　　1　　　2　　　3

A lone traveller can never be trusted.

In some areas of Luoland, the proverb is stated as:

Rienga jawuoth achiel.
　　3　　　1　　　2
An untrustworthy person travels alone.

The idea communicated is that he travels alone because no one trusts him and subsequently, because of that, he becomes even more lone. This same proverb may be stated with a morphological change on the word "Rienga" so that it becomes:

Oriengo jawuoth achiel.

These variations are so subtle and operate at the grammatical level. They do not invalidate the invariability feature.

Just to appreciate the brevity of proverbs, here is a list of proverbs in the original language and in English. The brevity should be appreciated in the light of the idea communicated that would otherwise ordinarily require more words.

61

Lak chogo.

The tooth is a bone.

(i.e. it knows no emotions and is seen in laughter even at times of sorrow.)

LUO

Msafiri kafiri.

A traveller is (as bad as) an unbeliever.

(i.e. he is sometimes compelled by circumstances to act contrary to his religion.)

SWAHILI

Kirihia thuti.

Desires tie

(i.e. If your desires be endless, your cares will be so too.)

GIKUYU

Looked at anatomically, proverbs display a variety of patterns which we now turn our attention to, namely:

(a) Abbreviation or ellipses

(b) Wellerism

(c) Parallelism

(d) Negative Axiom.

Abbreviation or ellipses

Abbreviation may not be so apparent especially when a proverb is written down. But in actual speech, there is always the tendency to give one part of the proverb and leave the second to be completed by the interlocuter either loudly or silently. Here are a few examples:

Speaker	Interlocuter
Chan man kowadu...	*ok moni nindo.*
Your brother's poverty...	does not prevent you from sleeping.

LUO

Chako chon...	*loyo dhi ajuoga.*
Starting early...	is better than going to the medicineman.

LUO

Asiyesikia la mkuu...	*huvunjika guu.*
He who doesn't listen to his elder...	breaks his leg.

SWAHILI

Kwenye miti...   *hakuna wajenzi.*
Where there are trees...   there are no builders.

SWAHILI

There is a second way in which proverbs are elliptical. This is the case of epigrammatical proverbs that are stated as single statements but which have longer unstated explanations behind them. Some two examples will illustrate the case.

Mbaka nyapong' gi dero.
The conversation between the grinding stone and the granary.

LUO

This proverb intends to explain a seasaw kind of struggle. The granary is alleged to have too much grain for the grinding stone to finish. Yet the latter is determined to turn it all into flour. The implicit conversation then is:

Granary: I am too large for you to finish.
Grinding stone: I will finish you with time.

The granary is confident that it will never be finished since its grains are always replenished when the new crop is harvested.

Era ilmoruak ong'wan.
There are four kinds of elders.

MAASAI

This proverb is an abbreviation of the following explanation:

Panyoneishu doesn't prepare for the future and therefore remains poor. Tanya ee has a little property but it is never increased. Olchanuki also has little property but is fortunate to live a long life and see his grandson circumcised. Orreteti is wealthy and popular, but does not have a long life as Olchanuki.

Both forms of abbreviation achieve certain effects. First they demonstrate to us the familiarity of proverbs so as to enable the audience to complete the blank parts. This, however, is not to say that everybody knows every proverb in his language. Those who do not know one learn it from the response of the others. Secondly, abbreviation ensures that the interlocutor is active and reinforces the speaker. It is therefore a style of enlivening the speech occasion.

Wellerism

This is the aspect of attributing the saying to some actual or fictional person with an introductory tag to authenticate the quotation. Sometimes the tag comes after the proverb. An example of wellerism is:

63

Etejoki opa, "Rrib-rrib kiyama, meeta nkonyek".
It has been said, "Marriage is 'rib-rib', it has no eyes".
(i.e. marriage is a matter of luck.)

MAASAI

The use of wellerism establishes objectivity. Whoever is saying the proverb attributes it to someone else and thus withdraws from the responsibility of its meaning. It is like saying: "I am not responsible for this but it is the truth that..."

Whereas we realise that some languages are very welleristic with their proverbs, it is not an explicit feature in all languages. In Swahili, wellerism seems to be implicit in all proverbs in that they are assumed to start *"Wahenga walisema"* – "The sages said". In this case the welleristic tag is optional and is in most cases left out, its use being according to the taste of the speaker.

Parallelism

This is the use of two balancing units within a literary form. It is quite a common feature in proverbs. Many proverbs exist in two parts usually of equal length, separated by a convenient punctuation mark. Parallelism makes the proverbs poetic and creates rhythm as we can see in the following proverbs:

Kukopa harusi, kulipa matanga.
Borrowing is a wedding, repaying a funeral.

SWAHILI

Baada ya kisa, mkasa; baada ya chanzo, kitendo.
After a reason, a happening; after a beginning, an action.

SWAHILI

Ciunagwo rūkomo, kīmenyi akamenya ikiunwo.
We speak by proverbs, he who is intelligent will understand.

GIKUYU

Man proposes, God disposes.

ENGLISH

Analytically, parallelism is manifested in a variety of ways. These are:

(a) Chiasmus or cross parallelism.
(b) Double proposition.
(c) Contrast proposition.

Chiasmus or Cross Parallelism

This is the repetition in the second part of a significant phrase that occurs in the first part of the proverb e.g.

> *Kwa muoga huenda kicheko na kwa shujaa huenda kilio.*
> With a timid person goes laughter, with a bold person goes wailing.
> (i.e. he who fights and runs away, lives to fight another day.)
> SWAHILI

> *Mũici wa mũthenya nĩ oĩo, na wa ũtukũ nĩ oĩo.*
> He who robs in the day is known and he who robs in the night is known.
> GIKUYU

In the second proverb there are some lexical omissions that may make the chiasmus not very apparent. Let us then stretch the proverb in its full structure to demonstrate the chiasmus.

> <u>*Mũici wa*</u> *mũthenya* <u>*nĩ oĩo,*</u> *na* <u>*mũici wa*</u> *ũtukũ* <u>*nĩ oĩo.*</u>

Double Proposition

This is the kind of parallelism where the first part of a proverb is a general statement while the second is its extension or usually its qualification. Both of them are affirmative in their interrelatedness.

> *Leo ni leo; asemaye kesho ni mwongo.*
> Today is today; he who says tomorrow is a liar.
> (One today is worth two tomorrows.)
> SWAHILI

> *Natuone ndipo twambie; kusikia si kuona.*
> Let us see then tell; hearing is not seeing.
> (Seeing is believing.)
> SWAHILI

> *Noong'u in' gora, kutuka miwal.*
> You eye, observe; you mouth, don't reply.
> MAASAI

> *Osina kishen; te naa ilmurran, nintaa minyi.*
> Suffering is a gift; if it is caused by warriors, make them your fathers.
> MAASAI

Gũkũra nĩ kũũru: ngathĩĩ ũrĩri ngĩcayaga.
It is bad to get old: (for) one goes to bed grumbling.
(Old mats want much patching.)

GIKUYU

Ndĩgũre: Konyũ kegũra nĩ koimirie ikwa.
Humble yourself: the inhabitants of Konyu were able to grow the yams after humbling themselves.

GIKUYU

In the sixth proverb, the explanation is in the story that:

The people of Konyu, a place in Kikuyu country, who had been at war with their neighbours of Mathira ceased to be raided and could till their fields in peace only by submitting.

As we notice from these proverbs, the first segment is the base of the proverb and the second is a reinforcement. The first part makes a declaration which is qualified in the second.

Contrast Proposition

In some proverbs the first part may be stated in the affirmative while the second in the negative or vice versa. This is what constitutes contrast proposition as in the examples below:

Kulea mimba si kazi, kazi ni kulea mwana.
It is not hard to-nurse a pregnancy; what is hard is to bring up the child.
(or: To nurse a pregnancy is not work; work is bringing up the child.)

SWAHILI

Umuwili waya, umutima tawila.
The body went, the heart did not go.

KAMBA

Negative Axiom

This is the statement in the negative of what may otherwise be put in the positive. The underlying positive sense is the axiom. We will take examples of the negative axioms and put in brackets the positive senses for clarity.

Gũtirĩ ngware nyinyi mahuriaini.
No partridge is small when it claws the soil.

66

(Axiom: Every partridge is big when it claws the soil.)

GIKUYU

Gũtirĩ ũkinyaga mũkinyĩre wa ũngĩ.
Nobody walks with another man's gait.
(Axiom: Everybody walks with his own gait.)

GIKUYU

Meeta emotonyi nemeiro ekenyua.
There is no bird that does not sing early in the morning.
(Axiom: Every bird sings early in the morning.)

MAASAI

Hapana marefu yasiyo na ncha.
There is no distance that has no end.
(Axiom: Every distance has an end.)

SWAHILI

After the structural aspects, we can look at the other devices in proverbs under the sub-titles:

(a) Mnemonics
(b) Imagery and allusion
(c) Humour.

Mnemonics

This refers to the sound effect that make an expression pleasant to hear and memorable especially as a result of the rhythm and musicality. Poetry, especially children's poetry and lyrical poems, heavily depend on mnemonic devices for effect. But mnemonics is not restricted to poetry alone. The devices are prevalent in all other genres. In this section we will look at the devices that contribute to the mnemonics of proverbs.

Alliteration

The recurrence of a consonantal sound in words that follow each other closely in a statement is what is technically called "alliteration". The sound may occur at the beginning, middle or any other part of the words although classically, it should be at the beginning. The following are proverbs that show this feature:

> *Jaber jaula.*
> All that glitters is not gold.

LUO

Jabudho e duonde ariyo jabed jamriambo.
He who stays in two "duonde" often becomes a liar.

LUO

N.B. *"Duonde"* is plural for *"duol"*. And *"duol"* is the hut in the homestead for the head of the home. He sits there in the evening beside a fire with the male children. The place is also used for discussion with other elders.

Hasira hasara.
Anger brings damage.

SWAHILI

Liandikwalo ndilo liwalo.
That which is written (by God) is what is (i.e. must surely come to pass).

SWAHILI

Chema chajiuza, kibaya chajitembeza.
A good thing sells itself, a bad thing advertises itself.

SWAHILI

Cia mūcii irī gacūgūma gacio gatathukagio nī mūthuri ūngī tiga mwene guo.
Home affairs have their staff, which cannot be brandished by anyone but the head of the house.

GIKUYU

Maaī maraitika matirī mūhītire.
Spilt water has no way of being collected.

GIKUYU

Assonance

It is the repetition of a vowel sound or their combination in words that come after one another or close together in a statement. The following proverbs show the aspect:

Ajidhaniye amesimama, aangalie asianguke.
He who thinks he has stood up, should be careful not to fall down.

SWAHILI

Kūrī ūkuū ūtatumwo, ta wa nyūngū.
There are things, like the earthen pot, which if ever broken, can't be repaired.

GIKUYU

Mwana mkaidi hafaidi mpaka siku ya Idi.
An obstinate child does not suffer save on the day of the festival.

SWAHILI

68

Ore oloany oltoilo loo Itung' anak nelo aning' ololmeneng' a.
He who denies the sound of the living will hear the sound of the dead.

MAASAI

Often, alliteration and assonance go hand in hand. A Swahili proverb like *"Mla nawe hafi nawe ila mzaliwa nawe"* is a beautiful combination of both. The proverb means "He who eats with you will not die for you but he that is born with you".

Rhime

In poetry, rhime means the similarity of sounds at the end of the lines. In proverbs, the concept more often refers to the case where a word about the middle of the line ends in the same sound as the last word in the line. This creates some phonic symmetry and enhances rhythm. It is called "Internal Rhime", e.g.

Haba na haba hujaza kibaba.
Little by little fills up the measure.

SWAHILI

Mtaka nyingi na saba hupata mwingi msiba.
He who boasts of his ancestry unduly will bring plenty of trouble upon himself.

SWAHILI

Man proposes, God disposes.

ENGLISH

Ideophone

An ideophone is a word that conveys its meaning through its sound. It is not semantically meaningful but its sound represents the idea. Here are two examples from Swahili.

Bandu – bandu huisha gogo.
Chip! Chip! Finishes the log.

SWAHILI

Chururu – si ndo! ndo! ndo!

SWAHILI

The meaning implied in the second case is that of a constant flow of water. "Chururu" signifies the gash while "ndo! ndo! ndo!"is the drip. Through the sounds we can in fact hear the gush and the drip.

Reduplication

This means the repetition of the same word or sound immediately after itself e.g.

>*Wat wat.*
>Kinship is kinship.

LUO

>*Chovya chovya yamaliza buyu la asali.*
>Constant dipping will empty a gourd of honey.

SWAHILI

>*Haraka haraka haina baraka.*
>Hurry hurry has no blessing.

SWAHILI

All these effects contribute immensely to the rhythm of the proverb. They create a euphony that improves the aesthetics of the proverb.

Imagery and Allusion

It is kind of imperative that effective literature uses figures of speech – images. The images conjure up in the mind pictures that reinforce the clarity of the subjects. Imagery is thus the oral graphics of literature.

Images may be tangible or abstract and indeed simple or complicated. They can be classified as similes, metaphors, personifications, symbols, e.t.c. We may also talk of tactile, visual, audio or olfactory images depending on the senses they appeal to.

Proverbs, like the other genres, are adept at the employment of figures scanning the spectrum of the physical, socio-cultural and political environment. The figures, once absorbed in literature, undergo a transformation by which they adapt an elevated identity and a representative significance. That then is one thing that foregrounds proverbial communication from all others and makes it literature.

In the next few pages we explore the nature of images in proverbs starting with stock names.

Many proverbs refer to names of people or places. The names get associated with the proverbial circumstances they refer to and hence gain a duality, i.e. they are realistic names and also belong to the world of fiction.

The factuality of the names hint at the probable historicity of the proverbs – the fact that the events may have actually happened. But then proverbs can also be coined out of imagination and use names and objects for immediacy of reference.

From the Luo we have the proverb: *"Nine gima ne Olweru oneno Nyayiera"* – "You will see what Olweru saw in Nyayiera". This is a proverb said to an overdaring person as a warning that he will face something dreadful and unpleasant. The focal images are Olweru and Nyayiera. Olweru is the name of a person and Nyayiera is that of a place. These names have become synonymous with the proverbial circumstances implied i.e. Olweru for the daredevil and Nyayiera for his undoing. They are stock allusions. It is not clear what it is that Olweru saw, nor is the author aware of the location of the place called Nyayiera. But that does not blur the pith of the proverb.

Some examples from the Gikuyu will give us more insight into the nature of proverbial allusions. The first is the famous:

> *Ciakorire Wacŭ mŭgŭnda.*
> The food found Wacŭ in the garden.

The proverb refers to the despised wife, Wacŭ, who went gardening while her husband was secretly holding a banquet for his favoured wife back at home. He had put a choice morsel to roast on the fire when a hawk swooped down and carried it away. The hawk got scalded by the hot morsel and dropped it, coincidentally in Wacŭ's garden. Thus she got a share of what she was being denied.

In context, the name Wacŭ is a stock allusion symbolic of those who are avenged by fate. In fact, that name occurs so many times in Gikuyu oral literature as a whole. For example it occurs in the following riddle:

> Challenge: They stampeded in Wacŭ's garden.
> Response: Floods.

A comparison of the proverb and the riddle show interesting parallels. First is the name 'Wacŭ', a reference to a presumably old woman. Secondly, the woman is associated with the garden, which also becomes a kind of stock allusion. And thirdly, the events are sort of fate oriented and out of man's control. Wacŭ seems to be all the time subject to fate and so we associate her with such phenomena.

Another Agikuyu proverb says:

> *Rŭrĩ na Komŭ rŭrĩ na Kaigŭ wa nyina.*
> If Komŭ has it, Kaigŭ, his brother has it too.

The names 'Komŭ' and 'Kaigŭ' denote brothers. They are randomly chosen by the originator of the proverb. But they could be any other names. However, here they are the denotations of brothers. One does not need to ask, "which Komŭ?" or "which Kaigŭ?" because they are stock references.

A rather similar example is in the Luo proverb:

71

Manga oromo gi Magare.
Manga has met Magare.

The proverb would be said of a person who has met his match. It is like saying that no one is invincible or in other words: "every dog has its day". Manga and Magare were inferably considered invincible until they met and acknowledged one another's strength.

The imagery of proverbs extends beyond the stock names and encompasses more from the general environment. It is to this that we now turn our attention to the world of plants where we get proverbs such as the following:

Gũciara kunaga irigũ ngingo.
The woman who gives birth to a child is like the banana tree that breaks under the weight of its fruit.

GIKUYU

Tonga si tuwi.
The juice of an immature coconut is not like the real coconut juice.

SWAHILI

The first proverb (simile) means that maternity is pain to the mother. The imagery is in the comparison with the banana tree. We all know how weighty the banana bunch is. The mother tree has the task of remaining erect even as it supports the bunch. The rapture of the child from the mother's womb is likened to the emergence of the bunch from the stem – what in this case is breaking the tree. The birth of a child is an added responsibility to the mother and she is forever weighed down by the child's needs. Quite often children turn out to be a headache to the parents and the latter almost begin to regret begetting them. The connotation in the image is, however, that no mother will abandon her maternal responsibility.

That kind of image is not a surprise from the Gikuyu, considering that they grow bananas. Neither is the second one from the coast where coconut is the predominant vegetation. In the second proverb the image is a comparison of what is potential and what is. It is the kind of proverb an elder politician may use to discard his younger opponent, implying that youth is a disqualification for some things.

The animal world is also a very rich source of imagery, as in the following:

Kuot Ogwal ok mon dhiang' modho.
The swelling of the frog does not prevent the cow from watering.

LUO

Simba mwenda kimya ndiye mla nyama.
The lion which moves silently is the one that eats meat.

SWAHILI

72

Otoyo moluor emaru.
It is the cautious hyena that lasts the night.

LUO

The first proverb derives from the physical environment where there is a supposed conflict between the frog and the cow. The former sees the water as its abode which must not be trespassed into. Unfortunately, the transgressor is more powerful and is undeterred by the "owner's" displeasure. So to say, the proverb sums up the hierarchical relationship between juniors and seniors. It is the same as "Might is right".

In the second example are animals drawn from the wildlife. It graphically presents what a lion does to get its prey. In order not to scare away the pray, it moves stealthily. The implication is that one who needs something has to be tactful and patient. A child who wants pocket money from the parent for example and declares that it is his right is likely not to get it. But the tactful one puts his case persuasively and waits for the response.

The last proverb is based on the experience that hyenas bombard kraals at night. The human beings at times lay traps. The hasty hyena that ambushes his way gets caught in the trap. But the one in the background lasts the night. The idea is that the coward lives to see another day while the brave lies dead in the field.

Let us now take some images from the domestic scene.

Pand nyaluo dhoge ariyo.
The traditional knife is double-bladed.

LUO

Thuol odonjo e koo.
A snake has entered the churning gourd.

LUO

In the first proverb, reference is made to the traditional knife as compared to the modern one which has a single blade. The former can cut in both directions. It is a comment on rumour mongers who create misunderstandings among people.

The churn is a very important item in the home. It is used for making milk sour and creating ghee, when it is shaken vigorously several times. The idea of a snake residing in it is therefore a dreadful one and leads to a big dilemma. Either the churn is left untouched in the hope that the snake will come out on its own, but at the risk of biting someone. Or else the gourd is broken and hence lost. The proverb is used in situations when there is something to lose both ways.

Another important source of proverbial imagery is the cultural practices of a people. We will take examples from the Gikuyu.

Mũndwithia rĩmwe ndagacoka kũndwithia rĩngĩ.

He who has circumcised me once does not return to do it again.

GIKUYU

Mwana mwende ndoĩ kũinia thũmbĩ.

The son most loved (by his parents) does not know how to shake his feather headdress.

GIKUYU

These two proverbs are based on the rite of circumcision. As put in the first one, it is a lifetime occasion and not recurrent on one person. And it is an unforgettable thing. The meaning of the proverb is that, one who has faltered once is the wiser for it. "Once bitten, twice shy". Or as the Chinese put it: "Fool me once, shame on you; fool me twice, shame on me".

The second case derides the attitude of not appreciating things that are got very easily. The son in the proverb is an embarrassment to his parents who have sacrificed to get him the choice headdress. He misconceives the essence of the trophy by carrying it passively on the head rather than putting it to use by shaking it.

Every aspect of life is a source of imagery. What strikes us is the aptness of the figures. The Luo talk about the double-bladed knife which occurs in their environment. The Agikuyu refer to circumcision, e.t.c. Thus we see that those creations are culturally based and determined. This kind of makes them a veil for the alien who needs to do some decoding to grasp the intended message.

For allusion, the reader is referred back to the section on classification.

Humour

Humour is one thing which makes a piece of communication irresistible to its audience whether intended by the speaker or incidental. The humour may arise from the words, images or just the context of usage.

Proverbs are quite full of humour. Being culturally based, it is easier for the native speaker of a language to discern the humour than for an outsider. This is because of the allusions and other paralinguistic nuances too subtle for recognition by the stranger. But all the same anyone with a sensitivity to literature should be able to appreciate humour whenever it occurs.

Humour is a convenient conveyance of satire. While we glee in laughter, we sometimes fail to recognise the criticisms in the expression. The humour then acts as a cushion in that we can choose to regard it at surface level. The following are some proverbs to lead to an explication of the humour in proverbs. Take the following Luo proverb for example:

Ng' ama chiemo gi muofu ema ong' eyo mit bor.
It is the man who eats with a blind man that knows the delicacy of a fatty morsel.

In this proverb, the Luo take a mirthful look at the tricky relationship between the seeing and the blind revellers. The former has the ability to choose the fatty pieces and leave the lean ones for the blind. This would not happen if both could see because then each would scramble for the best. It is not a wonder then that the Luo abuse the stout man saying: "You are as obese as he that eats with the blind man".

In the traditional society, there is a closely knit social fabric. Children are regarded as communal and treated as such. They are sent on errands and rewarded. The obedient one gets more rewards than the strong-headed one. Most of the rewards given are snacks eaten on the spot. By the end of the day, the child who has run so many errands will have eaten what is "equal to a mountain". The Luo summarise that in a humourous proverb as follows:

Nyathi mioro ema chiethne duong'
It is the child who runs errands that has bigger excrement.

The humour is in the fact that a hitherto unco-operative child may change so that he also gets bigger bog. As if the bigger the bog the more the prestige!

Another proverb that operates along the same frontiers is this Swahili one.

Amnyimaye punda adesi, kampunguzia mashuzi.
He who withholds lentils from a donkey reduces its passing of wind.

Apparently, lentils are a favourite food for a donkey. But the animal is unaware that this is the cause of its wind. The one who denies it the food appears to be an enemy while it is actually a saviour from the embarrassing excretive process. Here are some more humorous proverbs from the Agikuyu.

Mūgeni amīaga mbīrīra.
The foreigner evacuates in the cemetery for he does not know the place and its customs.

Mūici ndathiragwo nī marī hīndī.
The thief cannot keep fit because his stools contain undigested food.

These proverbs succeed in their humour by the graphic references they make. The foreigner can be visualised confidently striding into the cemetery to evacuate. A cemetery is a place held in awe and not one to be visited just any time. It is in fact believed that there are all sorts of spirits hovering around and which might turn malignant on the trespasser. Should the spirits decide that the act of evacuation there is a sign of disrespect, then one could imagine the kind of danger the stranger faces. And the second proverb ridicules the

75

thief who has to suffer perennial indigestion. By putting the case so crudely, the proverb appeals to people to strive for good health, at least by avoiding thievery.

It should now be easy to see the humour in these proverbs:

Jakuoth kiti.
The gossip never gets old (or never works).

LUO

Mũka ũrĩ kĩronda ainagĩra gĩtiro ihũgũ.
The woman who has a sore dances on the outskirts.

GIKUYU

Ndegwa nyinyi ĩhaicaga ng'ombe na mũtwe.
The young bull mounts the cows from the head.

GIKUYU

Kupanda mchongoma, kushuka ndio ngoma.
You may climb a thorn tree, but coming down again is a dance.

SWAHILI

Mwenye njaa hana miiko.
A hungry man observes no taboos.

SWAHILI

Mwenzako akinyolewa, wewe pia tia maji.
When your companion is being shaved, put water (on your head).

SWAHILI

SOCIAL FUNCTIONS OF PROVERBS

More often than not, scholars have confined themselves to what I call here the normative functions of proverbs i.e. being vehicles of advice, caution, warning, e.t.c. But proverbs serve more than that single area. The exploration that follows shows proverbs as both art and part of socio-culture.

Aesthetic Functions

The Nigerian novelist, Chinua Achebe has averred that "proverbs are the palm oil with which words are eaten". The Yoruba also have a metaphor that proverbs are the horses of communication. These sayings vividly point out that proverbs are a facilitator of verbal communication.

In both inter-personal and public speech, the speaker has two options: to say what he has to in a business-like way and bore his audience or to flower it and enthuse them. One who chooses the latter uses proverbs, rhetoric and anecdotes and achieves better communication. The communication becomes more enticing and persuasive. Let us illustrate this by quoting from Achebe's *Things Fall Apart*. This is the time when Okonkwo goes to ask for yams from Nwakibie. This is how he puts his case forward.

> I know what it is to ask a man to trust another with his yams, especially these days when young men are afraid of hard work. I am not afraid of work. The lizard that jumped from the high *iroko* tree to the ground said he would praise himself if no one else did. I began to fend for myself at an age when most people still suck at their mother's breasts. If you give me your yam seeds I shall not fail you.[13]

Okonkwo could have just gone and stated that he needed the yam seeds and made a solemn contract with Nwakibie to repay. He would have then bragged that his past spoke for itself. But he circumlocutes and praises himself in an acceptable way, using a proverb, a way that penetrates the heart of the old man. And he succeeds. Nwakibie responds in an equally artistic way:

> Eneke the bird says that since men have learnt to shoot without missing, he has learnt to fly without perching. I have learnt to be stingy with my yams. But I can trust you. I know it as I look at you. As our forefathers said, "You can tell a ripe corn by its look..."[14]

The proverb on the bird, Eneke, threatens to end on a refusal. But it is only to create suspense. The final agreement is slotted in with an approving proverb acknowledging Okonkwo's maturity. No one can doubt the aesthetic sense the proverbs have lent the dialogue. This is what they do in daily talk.

By means of proverbs and related linguistic facilities, the speaker achieves three things. He involves his audience by challenging their knowledge of their language; entertains them by introducing variety; and gets the message across more forcefully.

In actual speech, the audience responds instantly by nodding or doing some action that shows their attentiveness. The user of the proverbs has a way of sustaining that attention by abbreviating the proverbs and letting the audience complete them. The speech occasion is then made anti-phonal and lively.

But why is it that proverbs enable the speaker to make his point more forcefully? Because they are figurative and leave an indelible mark on the mind. The figures last longer in the mind than the accompanying junk words. This is because the listener may himself want to use them another time in a similar or different context. This adds to the flexibility of proverbs as now illustrated.

A social worker talking to parents on the need to discipline their children may start off with the proverb; "He who is not taught by his mother is taught by the world". In

77

common usage, the proverb castigates the child and exonerates the parent. But the social worker can twist it and ask the parents who would wish his child to be taught by the rough world. Therefore it is imperative for each parent to ensure discipline or otherwise prepare to feel the pangs of seeing their children wallowing in suffering at the cruel hands of the world.

Proverbs can be brought to our defence when in critical conditions. From *Things Fall Apart* again, note what Okonkwo says when he is scolded by Obierika for taking part in the abominable killing of Ikemefuna. He rationalises why the earth should not punish him by saying: "A child's fingers are not scalded by a piece of hot yam which its mother puts into his palm".

Undoubtedly, African writers have found proverbs as constant resources for enriching their works in the form of dialogue and even in direct narration. The latter can be illustrated from Achebe again:

> Everybody laughed except Okonkwo, who laughed uneasily, because, as the saying goes, an old woman is always uneasy when dry bones are mentioned in a proverb. Okonkwo remembered his own father.[15]

We can conclude here that proverbs are an enabling facility not only in African speech, but also in the writing. The knowledge of a large stock of proverbs makes one a formidable communicator.

Reflective Functions

Part of a society's oral literature today is inherited from the past and perpetuated by word of mouth. What we have now are the resistant precepts that have withstood the distortions and adaptations. As is obvious, whatever is transferred from the past undergoes some revision to refine and retain only that which is relevant today.

Proverbs are a summary of a people's philosophy of life, developed over generations of fluctuations. From the occurrences and recurrences, empirical conclusions are coined on the nature of life. These are expressed in proverbs as tested truths traversing the past via the present into the future. They have survived yesterday, apply today and guide the pathway of tomorrow. The refinement of proverbs has occurred through reflections on man's nature, what he has done, what he is doing and what he is capable of doing. To say then that they play a reflective role is to mean that they give an insightful sense of probabilities. They act as mirrors through which we glance at the society, its attitudes and thought processes.

Although we may not always be able to trace the history of proverbs, it exists as far as we accept that proverbs are not composed in a vacuum. Our inability to trace the history may be a result of the lack of documentation in pre-literate Africa and the pre-occupation with the utility of proverbs rather than their etymology. The modern man therefore finds himself at a loss with many of his community's stock which are full of archaisms and which as a result just sound empty words to him.

At this point, let us appraise the speculative function of proverbs as statements of past truth and as they apply today.

Kinship is a revered institution in Africa. Regardless of all sorts of differences, blood relationship remains an inescapable obligation. A Maasai proverb expresses this idea viz:

Eiu oltung' ani osuuji naa olanya.
A man's son may be a coward but he is still his son.

The Maasai are a gallant pastoral community that highly value bravery. A father is most embarrassed by a cowardly son. But he cannot disown him. If we apply the science of genetics, the father's recessive genes may have been responsible for the son's cowardice.

Taking a glance at another aspect of life, we get the following proverb from the Luo:

Ogwang' tho e lo wadgi.
A mongoose dies in the stead of its brother.

A mongoose is loathed as a scavenger on poultry and so there is always a vigil for any mongoose roving around. Once it is spotted, it is hunted down and hit for having disappeared with so many hens. The truth, however, is that a different mongoose may have been the culprit.

Quite truly, this is a phenomenon we see in the criminal world. Where there is a wily and notorious thief, any suspect gets badly clobbered in the belief that he is the perpetrator of the past cases although he may not be. And the idea can be observed in many other facets of life where people suffer not because they are guilty but because they are found on the spot.

Here are now proverbs that relate closely to the economic world.

Meitopir enelikae iltuli aare.
The property of another cannot fatten two buttocks.

MAASAI

Mbũri yene mũitha nĩ gũtũ.
The best part of another's goat is the ear.

GIKUYU

Dher ariembo wuongo nyiedho to ng'iyo oko.
The custodian of a loaned cow milks it while looking out.

LUO

79

The Maasai are stating the truism that one cannot glee on another's property. Whatever access one has to it, the owner has precedence and the other person can be dispensed with any time. The Agikuyu state that an outsider should not expect a choice morsel and should be content with an inferior part, the ear. And the Luo recreate the unreliability of loans. The owner of the cow can come for it any time and so the loanee is never sure of his milk the next day. So he looks out to see if the owner is on the way so as to stop milking and prepare the cow for departure. Alternatively, he does not want to be accused by the owner of overmilking the cow.

These are proverbs that apply very aptly to the economics of export and foreign aid. Foreign aid is always given with strings attached. The giver knows what he stands to gain in the stake. The recipient should not then bask in the comfort of such aid as it may end up making him poorer.

The unpredictability of international relationships makes reliance on foreign aid dangerous. Coups and changes in political leadership can make hitherto friendly nations bitter enemies. If there was a flow of aid it is most likely to be cut. The recipient is then put in a most awkward position. In other words, he can easily be blackmailed.

Coming to export trade, we have always heard that African and other third world countries export the best parts of their produce and leave the lowest quality bit for domestic consumption. This dumps their standards of living. Rationally, it should be the other way round. A prudent person will not give out his best and retain the worst for his family if he really minds their welfare. This is what the Agikuyu proverb is telling us.

And more proverbs can be quoted on the reflective functions.

Normative Functions

Proverbs are largely didactic. They are used to point out facts of life where there is an anomaly so as to restructure things and to prompt the deviant back to normality. This presupposes a certain standard way of behaviour that is desirable and should be maintained. Hence proverbs are used to warn, caution, advise, lampoon, console, encourage, e.t.c. These are what we refer to here as the normative functions of proverbs.

But as already stated, a proverb can be multi-contextual in application. If in our analysis below we regard a proverb as advisory, that does not make it unusable for any other purpose. Here then are some of the normative functions of proverbs with examples.

General Counsel:

> *Janeko ema lielore kende.*
> It is only the mad man who cuts his own hair.
>
> LUO

80

We are being counselled on the value of interdependence. We must complement one another and doing otherwise is an insanity.

Advise:

> *Toisho mime.*
> Give birth without pain i.e. tolerate your children's mistakes.

MAASAI

Caution:

> *Akuru ok kuodh e iro.*
> The dove is never backbitten in smoke.

LUO

The proverb is meant to caution a careless talker that there could be a spy among the people he is talking to. As the English say, "Even walls have ears".

Warning:

> *Meitalang' elipong' oltung'oni ilkejek aare.*
> A female does not make a man cross two rivers.

MAASAI

This is a warning to a man who marries a woman who has run away from another man. He is being told that she may as well leave him also.

Admonition:

> *Tiga kũonia ngarĩ kũhaica mũtĩ.*
> Stop teaching the leopard how to climb a tree (i.e. Don't teach your grandmother how to knit).

GIKUYU

This could be said to an impudent child who presumes he can even advise his elders.

Criticism:

> *Mũtĩ ũtagũtemwo ndũgerekagĩrĩrĩo ithanwa*
> A tree which is not intended to be felled, is not aimed at with an axe.

GIKUYU

The proverb criticises a person who over-applies himself to a task or overburdens himself with too many pursuits.

Consolation:

Teke la kuku halimwumizi mwanawe.
A hen's kick does not hurt her chick.

SWAHILI

The idea is that parents are benign and would not do what would harm their offspring. Or, ones own does not seek to destroy him.

And so the list can go on.

Summative Functions

Some scholars have classified proverbs as "short forms" and others as "gnomic forms". The gist of these categorisations is that proverbs are brief. The second categorisation however gives us the dimension of proverbs being veiled in their meaning. Thus we can combine the two ideas and say that proverbs are both short and shortening. How?

Whereas there are general interpretations to each proverb, a proverb may be used in fresh contexts when it acquires a fresh meaning. In a way then, one can never generalise and rush to conclusions whenever he hears a familiar proverb without stopping to analyse the context of usage. Proverbs are a kind of code language. Specialists in their usage can deliberately employ rare ones to cut out amateurs from their conversation.

Proverbs are also condensations of larger issues. This makes them veiled and require decoding for a stranger to understand them. We have in earlier chapters seen how there are elaborate explanations behind some proverbs. For example, there is the Maasai proverb about the four kinds of elders; Panyoneishu (carefree), Tanya ee (lazy), Olchanuki (long life) and Orreteti (wealthy and popular).

The summative function is also evident in narratives. Didactic tales explicitly or implicitly end with some proverbs as a summation of the moral. Here is a paraphrase of a Yoruba narrative with such a summation.

> In a town called Irandunwo, lived a loose talker called *"Elenuobere"* – "sharp mouth". One day it was rumoured that a man had seduced the Oba's wife. He went and said he had designed the plan by which that act was accomplished. He was taken to court and convicted of talking rubbish hence fined one pound and five shillings. He had no money and so went to prison.
>
> But a kind farmer agreed to bail him out if he would work on his farm for five days. The next day on the way to the farm, they heard a sound in the bush. Elenuobere burst out, "Surely that is a horse grazing, and its left eye is blind". The farmer betted with him that if that was true he would strike off five shillings from the debt. If not, the debtor would give one extra day of work. When they

reached the animal, Elenuobere was proved right and so his debt was reduced.

Soon afterwards they came across a wet spot and he claimed it was the piss of a pregnant woman. Once again he was right and the debt was reduced. At the farm when they sat to eat, the farmer sighed three times and each time Elenuobere claimed he knew what was in his thoughts. The argument that ensued led them to the king's court for a settlement, the farmer all the time confident that he could deny whatever Elenuobere would say.

Before the royal assembly, Elenuobere then stated: "The first thought was: May God Almighty give long life to the king. Your second thought was : May this royal family continue to rule long in our town. And your third thought was: May God grant that the King's heir will rule after him". The whole gathering, including the farmer affirmed saying "Amen". He could not deny lest he annoyed the king.

Elenuobere got his acquittal and relief from the labour. "The mouth that commits an offence must talk itself out of punishment".[16]

The story illustrates the quoted final adage. Across East Africa we get proverbs with the same meaning e.g.

Ulimi hauna mfupa.
The tongue has no bone (it can get round anything both literally and metaphorically).

SWAHILI

Meeta olng' ejep erubata.
The tongue has no joint.

MAASAI

It can come to its defence at times of difficulty through lies, denials, e.t.c.

The two proverbs above sensitise us to the comparison one can undertake of proverbs bearing the same meaning from different communities and from the same community. See the following from different communities:

Kinda e teko.
Persistence is strength.

LUO

Bandu bandu huisha gogo.
Chip chip finished the log.

SWAHILI

Mbĩa iminaga ndarwa na igũtha.
The mouse finishes the hide by gnawing.

GIKUYU

83

Little strokes fell great oaks.

And some from the same community as in the following Luo proverbs:

Jopuonj mang' eny ne oketho Kabete.
Many teachers spoilt Kabete.

Oyieyo mang' eny ok kuny bur.
Many rats do not dig a hole.

They correspond to the English "Too many cooks spoilt the broth".
From Swahili, we get this set of three:

Bandu bandu huisha gojo.
Chip chip finished the log.

Haba na haba hujaza kibaba.
Little by little fills the measure.

Chovyo chovyo humaliza buyu la asali.
Constant dipping will empty a gourd of honey.

Incidentally, there are proverbs which oppose one another, hence showing the complexity of realities that they deal with or which pertain in the communities they originate from. For example, there are these two from Swahili:

Baba wa kambo si baba.
A step-father is not a father.

Mume wa mama ni baba.
A husband of a mother is a father.

Whereas the first proverb negates the essence of a step father, the second seems to restore it on the grounds that as the inheritor of the mother, he is as good as a father.

Finally, it is essential to note that proverbs, like other genres, respond to change in a process in which new proverbs are coined. The following two expressions, for example, have become proverbial among the Luo:

Chuth ber.
Immediacy is best.

Kama itiye ema ichieme.
It is from where you work that you eat.

The first expression was popularised by a political campaigner who said he believed in giving development instantly and not promising his constituents that he would do so on getting to parliament. So he gave his supporters gifts to solicit their votes. The expression is now used in other contexts where people want the consideration in their contracts fulfilled immediately.

The second expression means to say that a person derives his livelihood from where he works and so should take the job very seriously. But there are other unethical undertones in it. A corollary saying that has developed alongside it says:

> *Kama ichieme ema itiye*
> It is where you eat from that you work in.

The reversal of the saying means to imply that a person will only have a reason to stay in a place where he derives some benefit.

Such sayings are subtle developments that may go unnoticed and which it is necessary to document.

NOTES

1. The diagram is taken directly from Roger D. Abraham's "The Complex Relations of Simple Forms" in *Folklore Genres*, ed. Dan-Ben Amos, Austin: University of Texas Press, 1976.
2. Anthony Castle. *Quotes and Anecdotes*, St Paul's Publications: Bombay, 1983.
3. Ibid.
4. Ruth Finnegan, *Oral Literature in Africa*, Oxford University Press: Nairobi , 1970, p. 433-4.
5. Ibid. p. 400.
6. A. O. Massek and J.O. Sidai, *Wisdom of Maasai*, TransAfrica Publishers: Nairobi, 1974.
7. Ibid.
8. Ibid.
9. Ibid.
10. Chinua Achebe, *Things Fall Apart*, Heinemann: London, 1958, p. 151 (1978 edition).
11. Peter Seitel. *Proverbs: A Social Use of Metaphor* in Dan-Ben Amos (ed), Folklore Genres, Austin: University of Texas Press, 1978.
12. Ibid.
13. Achebe, op.cit. p.16.
14. Ibid.
15. Ibid. p. 15.
16. The unabridged version of the story appears in Ulli Beier's *Not Even God is Ripe Enough*, Heinemann: London, 1968, p. 5-7.

GENERAL NOTES

The author has extensively relied on the undernoted sources for examples of proverbs used in the text and their explanations.

1. For Maasai proverbs: A. O. Massek and J. O. Sidai, *Wisdom of Maasai*, TransAfrica Publishers: Nairobi, 1974.

2. For Luo proverbs: Paul Mboya, *Luo Kitgi gi Timbe' i*, Anyange Press: Kisumu, 1938 and the author's own collection from a research conducted in Asembo-Bay in 1983/84.

3. For Agikuyu proverbs: G. Barra, *1000 Kikuyu Proverbs*, Kenya Literature Bureau: Nairobi, 1987.

4. For Swahili proverbs: S. S. Farsi, *Swahili Sayings 1*, Kenya Literature Bureau: Nairobi, 1982.

PART THREE
ORAL POETRY

"We sing when we fight, we sing when we work, we sing when we love, we sing when we hate, we sing when a child is born, we sing when death takes a toll."

Osadebey, D. C. et al, "West African Voices", *African Affairs 48, 1949*.

What is Poetry?

Poetry is the expression of powerful human feelings (emotions), thoughts and ideas using words and sounds arranged in the best possible manner. The arrangement in the best possible order is called **verse**. Therefore poetry can straight·away be defined as the use of versified language to express human feelings, thoughts and ideas.

Verse and poetry are not the same. Verse can exist without poetry, but poetry depends on verse for form and appeal. Poetry is distinguished from verse by the depth of feelings, thoughts and ideas. Words devoid of these remain as verse however well arranged they may be.

What is Oral Poetry?

Following from the general definition of poetry, oral poetry then is the verbal expression of feelings, ideas and thoughts using versified language.

In the analysis of oral poetry, there is often a confusion between poetry and song. These two are not exactly the same. Song is just one way of delivering poetry. A poem may be sang, declaimed or recited. Like verse, song may be devoid of poetry: it may not convey any feelings, thoughts or ideas and may be nothing but a set of sounds set to a tune. Song is not always poetry and poetry is not always song. As we even realise in written poetry, not everything that is centred on a page is poetry. Poetry must have recognisable forms and motifs of thematic relationships and development to integrate words and sounds from their nominal value to verse and finally to poetry.

CHARACTERISTICS OF ORAL POETRY

Certain features of performance and style mark out oral poetry from written poetry. The two actually share a lot of features and only differ mainly on the performance of oral poetry. The difference can be seen by highlighting the features of oral poetry.

Performance

The following features in the performance of oral poetry are distinctive.

Oral Delivery

The oral poem is principally composed and rendered using word of mouth.

Dependence on Suprasegmental Features of Language

These are the non-graphic aspects of language like tone and pitch which characterise especially African languages. Through tone and pitch, a varying mood and meaning can be established using the same words or set of words. For instance, the Luo word "kuoyo" can mean "to sew" or "sand" depending on the tone used.

Elasticity and Spontaneity

In oral performance, especially of song, the text is often not fixed. It may be shortened or lengthened depending on the requirements of the moment. The lengthening may be done by repeating certain lines or inclusion of other ideas. Often an oral performer takes stock of his audience in the performance and uses it as a source of reference by including their names and other things observed there during the performance. It means that as he performs, he also creates; it is not a mere reproduction of rehearsed material. The expansive aspect is what we refer to here as 'elasticity' while the ability to incorporate new matter extemporaneously comprises the spontaneity.

Antiphony

This is the call and response structure. The classic example of an antiphonal delivery is the existence of a soloist who calls the tune and the rest chorus the response. But there are variations in this structure where for example, the two parties are complementing one another rather than the soloist dominating in calling the tune.

Public Rendition

Most oral poetry is performed to an audience making it a public affair. Only in a few circumstances can we talk of "private" poetry e.g. a lover singing her boyfriend's song on her way to the river.

Dramatisation

This is the use of body, face and movement to reinforce the words and voice. It may be elaborate with big gestures and wide movements over space or fairly limited to nodding the head, stamping the feet and clapping while in a stationary position. It is inconceivable that a poem would be delivered without any form of drama, as defined.

Accoutrements and Instruments

This refers to the attire of the performer and other physical paraphernalia. These aspects are particularly significant in song performance. The wearing of a headgear, colourful skins and the production of sounds from instruments like the drum, jingles, horn and the lyre enhance the audio reception and act as visual attractions to the audience.

Style

Repetition

This is the recurrence of a mood, idea, sound, word or line in a poem. The most conspicuously repetitive feature of oral poems are the words, lines or sets of lines coming regularly after each stanza – the refrains. But there are varieties of repetition. Repetition helps mainly in the establishment of mood and themes.

Mnemonic Devices

These are the sound effects that enhance the cadence of the poem. They include:

Alliteration:	The recurrence of an initial consonantal sound in words that come close together in a line.
Assonance:	The repetition of a vowel sound in words that occur close together in a line.
Rhime:	The similarity of sounds in words that occur in the same position in two or more lines. The most talked of rhime is the end-rhime, where two or more words at the end of different lines end in the same sound. Although technically a word does not rhime with itself, in oral poetry it is common to find the same word at the end of several lines in a stanza producing a rhiming quality.
Ideophone:	The use of sound-words i.e. words which have no semantic sense but contribute to the structure and rhythm of the poem.
Rhythm:	The patterned rise and fall of sounds and words in a poem. Each poem has its rhythm which facilitates the appeal to the ear, danceability and general reception.

Use of imagery and local idioms

Oral poems heavily draw their reference from the indigenous environment of their creation and hence abound in local imagery. Reference, for example, to a lover's teeth being as white as fresh milk attests to the pastoralist environment.

Turning to idioms, each language has its wealth of combination of words to signify different ideas. Instead of talking about "my wife", someone would idiomatically talk of "the daughter of my mother-in-law". Such periphrases and other idiomatic expressions are significantly present in many oral poems.

Poetic Composition: Populism or Specialism?

Who in any given society, composes poems? Is poetic composition a specialist (separatist) or populist (communal) art? In what ways?

Folklorists, who are mainly concerned with the sociological value of oral traditions, believe that oral compositions are communal creations with no acknowledged individual authors. This position insinuates that everybody is a poet or at least has the potential to be one.

Contrary to this, one can strongly contend that each poem is originally composed by an individual or group of individuals and that they are not just emanations from the culture. The point is that not everyone is or can be a poet.

Populism in poetic performance, and claimed for poetic composition, may be a case of transferring the romantic picture of ancient Africa as a mass of egalitarianism where the individual was secondary to the community. It is true that in primal society, preoccupation was with the functionality of poetry rather than authorship. By the very nature of an oral poem, it gains wide accessibility to a large public and gets transmitted "like bush fire" in a sense that makes it more public than private.

The nature of performance of most oral poems may strengthen the populist argument. Antiphonal, choral and orchestral performances depend on the learning and delivery of poems by more than one person. The success of the art ensues from the contribution of all. More so, a poem can be varied and adopted to different words and meanings completely diverse from the original text by the incumbent performers. It therefore adapts a new identity and goes beyond the probable author. In such genres as lullabies, play songs and work songs, the element of performance completely subsumes that of authorship.

What about the case of poetry as a specialist art. Finnegan gives us very lucid examples of specialisation in the art of poetic composition and performance. She talks of the formally trained Rwanda bards, charged with the "delivery and preservation of the dynastic poems whose main object was to exalt the king and other members of the royal line". She says:

> A court poet was known as Umusizi w'umwami (dynastic poet of the king). This category included a number of poets, both those with the inspiration and skill to compose original works and those (the bards) who confined themselves to learning and reciting the compositions of others. The court poets have always had their own association – the Umutwe w'Abasizi, "band of dynastic poets" – comprising those families officially recognised as poetic.[1]
>
> The poems themselves were exceedingly elaborate and sophisticated, with specialised mode of expression mastered only by the intelligentsia of the society.

The style was full of archaism, obscure language and highly figurative terms of expression.[2]

Continuing to comment on this, she gives the description of the training of the youth in the art of memorisation and recitation, as a means of identifying future poets.

> Among the Rwanda, somewhat unusually, part of the production of the Oral Literature was through memorisation of received versions of the poems, and the attribution of personal authorship was the rule rather than the exception... and there seems to have been a conscious effort to preserve the exact words of the text.[3]

This is evidence that poetry can be a very specialistic art, a preserve of the few talented ones whom the others can only imitate. Part of this restriction, among the Rwandese, is in the fact that the dynastic poets were trained especially to recite the poetry among their contemporaries and to the king only.

Specialism can also be viewed from the aspects of apprenticeship and inheritance. A talented youth may be attached to a reknown poet to learn the art of poetry. Even in many musical groups today, a fellow starts off as a member of a larger troupe to gain skill and experience before striking out on his own.

Inheritance is easily corroborable. In an effect to preserve the art of the family, a father-poet may deliberately choose and train a son to perpetuate it. In certain cases, one may not even rule out the possibility of genetic inheritance. While conducting research at Mabinju village in Siaya District in 1983/84, the author encountered the case of Zablon Okome Onyango, a composer and singer of praise poems, and his son Fanuel Abong'o who was leading a group of traditional singers calling themselves 'Mabinju Jazz Band'. The group specialised in composing and singing dirges although they also performed praise poems especially in honour of politicians during campaigns.

Finnegan cites two other examples of specialist poetry in the case of Ethiopian 'dabteras' and Yoruba Ifa priests. The dabteras composed 'qene' – a short witty poem:

> ... marked by great obscurity of style, extreme condensation, delight in the use of puns and an abundance of metaphors and religious allusions. In keeping with their highly specialised nature, the qene demanded prolonged intellectual training of their mastery, and we hear of schools of rhetoric designed to train poets in the art of qene composition.[4]

And of the Yoruba Ifa priests:

> The Ifa diviners (babalawo – father of mysteries) spend several years learning the literature for their profession. The minimum seems to be three years: the first is often spent learning the names and structure of the odu, the second and third

learning some of the literature of each as well as the actual practice of divination and its rituals.[5]

Any activity that requires training is by that fact specialist. The cases of the Rwandese, Ethiopian and Yoruba poets illustrate the fact that certain genres in these societies are restricted and require professional training.

Okot p'Bitek has interesting revelations about authorship of poems. Dismissing the folkloristic belief in communal composition, and emanation of poetry, he says: "children compose their own poems and are their own choreographers"[6].

But he later gives a hint that there was specialism in composing poems among the Acholi of Uganda in the following words:

> The Nanga players are the main composers of music and poems in Acholiland. But other poets compose their songs using other instruments or none at all. The famous Nanga players have a large repertoire of original compositions. They also learn other men's songs and transform them so that they sound almost original.[7]

The idea that Nanga players are the "main" composers depict poetry as a specialist art. But the bit of adopting other men's songs and having theirs adopted as well, in the ultimate end, puts poetry as a communal art if the art that is transmitted through generations has been shaped by different poets and continues to be so.

In other words there seems to be a mutual co-existence of specialism and populism in Acholi poetry. The case is even more evident in the case of 'mwoc'.

> Mwoc are short poems an individual shouts at certain critical moments. During a quarrel, when a person is highly provoked he shouts his mwoc and the fight begins at once and during the fight, he shouts his praise names on hitting or spearing or throwing down his opponent. In a hunt, the mwoc is shouted by the person who spears an animal...
>
> There are two kinds of mwoc, one which belongs to a particular individual alone, and the other which belongs to the chiefdom. Every Acholi male has his own mwoc, and many but not all women have theirs too. It usually arises from some funny incident.[8]

Okot goes on to cite how he composed his own mwoc. He and his mother had gone to visit a woman called Agik. When the host had put the pot of water on the fire for millet bread, she went to beg flour from her co-wife in vain. In shame she burst out wailing. Hence Okot's mwoc runs:

> She hoped that her co-wife had some flour;
> She saw her co-wife return from Parabongo
> And thought she had bought some flour and yeast;

You visit your home frequently;
You fall into the inner room crying.[9]

The fact that each individual composes his own poem means that everyone has the poetic facility hence poetic composition is not a separatist art. The chiefdom mwoc is described thus:

> The chiefdom mwoc is shared by all members of the chiefdom, and is also shouted by wives of that group, except when the situation is such that her loyalty to her people is at stake...
>
> These poems often embody names of chiefs of old, ...mountains and rivers – sites once occupied by the chiefdom, fierce beasts or harmful plants, e.t.c. which are supposed to exhibit or represent the characteristics or quality of the people of the chiefdom; or thus may contain slogans, telling what the chiefdom has been: its strength and glory, e.t.c.[10]

Although Okot does not say who composed these mwoc of the chiefdoms, it is surmisable that they were the accomplished poets. And then the legacy of transmitting them over generations and being shared by everybody makes them communal poetry, a tendency towards populism.

From Okot we see the co-existence of the specialist and the populist. This is also a case seen in the 'impango' compositions of the Zambian woman. 'Impango' is a woman's personal praise song that she sings at beer parties or at work. How is it composed?

> Impango composition is known to be very difficult, and in every village there are a few women who are specially skilled in this art. What happens when a woman wants to make an 'impango' is that she first thinks out the rather lengthy words – it may be in praise of herself, her lover or her husband and then calls in some of her women friends to help her. Together they go to a well-known maker of 'impango' songs. After hearing the woman's ideas, she then, often over a period of several days, composes the complete tune for the whole song. She calls a party of women to practise it each evening after supper, and they continue until the 'impango' is complete and has been mastered by the whole party. The group is then disbanded and the woman who 'owns' the song continues to sing it on her own, knowing that if she forgets at any point she can ask one of the practice party to help her.[11]

This instance clearly illustrates that poetry may not be so separatist as to be exclusive of communal composition . Note that the woman is not only helped to compose the words but also to sing the song, and the specialist is brought in to perform musical and poetic refinement.

94

From this survey, we can conclude that specialism or populism in poetic composition and performance differs with communities. In some there is overt training leading to specialisation and elitisisation of the poets. But in others, and with many genres of poetry, there is no restriction on composers. And the fact that poems can be adopted by others tend to communal ownership. In a way then, poetry is both specialist and populists in as far as there is need to acknowledge individual authors, and also in as far as the poems become public property on performance and in many cases involve more than one person.

CLASSIFICATION OF ORAL POETRY

This section looks at the categorisation of poetry by listing some of the common terms used in labelling poems, out of them analysing the criteria used and also exemplifying.

Terms Used in Classifying Oral Poetry

The terms that follow are commonly found in oral literature texts in connection with poetry:

Birth or Cradle songs: performed during the occasion of a birth.

Circumcision songs: performed during the season or ceremony of circumcision in communities which observe the rite.

Marriage/Wedding/Nuptial songs: performed during marriage ceremonies.

Dirges or Elegiac poetry: sung or recited at funerals or during memorial rites.

Beer party songs: performed by either the revellers or a poet at a beer drinking party.

Work songs: performed as accompaniment to some chores like ploughing, weeding, fishing, pounding, e.t.c.

Hunting poetry: performed by hunters as prelude to, during or after a hunting expedition or any other occasion that brings hunters together.

War poetry: performed principally by warriors before, during or after war.

Love songs: based on romance.

Political songs: recitals or songs whose subject is politics or politicians.

Topical songs: composed about contemporary affairs as running commentaries on social affairs especially cultural transition.

Lyric: short poem meant to be sung or generally a poem expressing deep personal feelings.

Panegyric: praise poetry.

Court poetry or Official poetry: performed by accomplished poets at kings' palaces especially in praise of the leader.

Epic or Heroic poetry: elaborate poems based on the lives of heroes, describing their birth, growth, exploits or death and generally surveying historical events in a people's past.

Hortatory Poetry: meant to encourage.

Satirical poetry: meant to criticise or debase an individual, act or institution.
Elocutionary poetry: not principally concerned with serious messages but set to play on the art of language and expressiveness.

One immediately notices that these terms apply along a slide rule kind of system e.g. when we talk of a praise song, a variety of performances/poems could be denoted. For example, a lullaby may praise the child; a dirge may praise the dead; a wedding song may praise the bride and the groom and a war poem the war hero. Praise therefore is a functional aspect that permeates many poems.

Another nebulous term is "Topical songs". Topicality is an aspect of time. A poem is topical because of the currency of its content. As soon as the subject becomes stale, the topicality of the song disappears. In which case, all topical songs become historical. Okot p'Bitek sums up the transitory nature of oral poetry when he talks about the Orak love dance in the following words:

> Being running commentaries on current affairs of the individual and the group, the songs of the orak dance soon become out of date and unfashionable; and new ones, equally transitory, are composed to replace them.[12]

The discussion of the expression "topical songs" reminds one of the other expression "contemporary poetry", an expression used to refer to compositions of today, rendered in the poetic mode but dealing with distinctly topical issues. The often quoted example of such poetry are what are otherwise called "pop music".

In certain circles, there is reluctance to acknowledge that such compositions are no less oral literature than those of the past, the so-called traditional. That could be a mentality arising from the stereotyped treatment of oral literature as belonging to the past. But the fact is that oral literature, and poetry for that matter, exists now and is adapting in form and content to today's social environment. Thus the prime concern should be with the examination of these pieces for their poetry rather than relegating them to a lesser status because the singers or poets use modern electronic equipment and deal with topical rather than classical issues.

In this regard, poetry can be seen to have gained a triptych identity in the current society with the distinctive categories being traditional, choral and pop poetry i.e. there is a strong presence of traditional compositions as of the Luo Nyatiti player; then there is also the strong emergence of choir-type performances as in schools' festivals; and finally there are the ubiquitous pop musicians especially in the towns. One would find that these types of performances in their own right use varieties of poetic styles including interjection, parody, metaphor and idiom.

But however nebulous or controversial the terms are, they still reveal criteria which can be used to classify poetry, a general topic to which we now turn.

Criteria for Classifying Oral Poetry

The breakdown that follows is a summary of guidelines that could be and are used to classify oral poetry.

Traditional Classification

In this approach, oral poems are classified according to how the source community groups them. It is a field work oriented approach and a handy example is what Kabira and Mutahi do in *Gikuyu Oral Literature* in which they talk of such categories as:

- *Nyĩmbo cia irĩgũ* (songs for uncircumcised girls)
- *Nyĩmbo cia ihĩĩ* (songs for uncircumcised boys)
- *Nyĩmbo cia aanake* (songs for young men)
- *Nyĩmbo cia airĩtu* (songs for young women)
- *Nyĩmbo cia atumia* (songs for women)
- *Nyĩmbo cia athuuri* (songs for old men)

This classification system follows the parameters of the performer of the song in terms of age and sex. It is what we have referred to elsewhere as **personal criterion**. This is not to say, however, that every traditional classification system follows the same pattern. From the research point of view, this approach tries to capture exactly how the community groups its material, which should be the starting point for any researcher intent on classifying the collected material in any other way.

Thematic Criterion

The theme or subject of a poem may be used to classify it. Such terms as 'religious poetry', 'dirges', e.t.c. derive from the themes of the poems. Here is an example of a love song.

> **Love Song** *by Mopoi*
> When could your praises be sang, Ololtibili?
> For this scorching summer heat prevent it
> They cannot be sung at midday
> For then the sun weakens the cattle
> They cannot be sung at sunset
> For the sun will set with the praises

Oh, when the sun gets to that point
(pointing to the position of the sun at about 9 a.m.)
Praises of he with the scarlet one will be sung.

I developed admiration for you
Not at the drinking hall
I have stored the love of my love
Since I was just a little girl
I have stored it at the gall bladder
To nurture it day and night

I dare not store this precious love of my love
At the head, for the mind abounds with changes
It has edged between the fingers and the palm
As well as the spleen and the liver
The love of my love has gone down
To where the infants lie
I store it where the infants are carried
To keep it growing day by day.

He that detests my loving the warriors
Find one tough thing to do
Scrape the road with your buttocks
Until you have reached Nairobi
Put a hyena at the sheep pen
As well as the slain beast (cheetah)
If by morning the sheep are safe
I will give up the brother of Talash
Then you can.bleed the whitenosed one (donkey)
To purge me from the long-haired one.[13]

MAASAI (Kenya)

In this poem a woman expresses her strong love for a man and challenges the jealous husband to perform impossible tasks if he really insists she must forsake the illicit affair. It is therefore thematically a love song.

But on the other hand, a moralist may see the theme as infidelity rather than love. This is to raise the point that thematic classification is actually very subjective. What I may see as the thematic emphasis of a poem may differ from someone else's view. In any case most poems tend to be multi-thematic. Consider the poem that follows:

98

We Women Will Never Have Peace

We women will never have peace,
We will never prosper, the troubles from men are ceaseless,
At night they are worse.
He stands his bicycle,
He calls me, I respond,
My man hurls insults at my mother;
The troubles from men are ceaseless,
At night they are worse.
He drinks to his full,
And vomits on me;
When shall we have peace?
The troubles from men are ceaseless,
My house is spotlessly clean,
My man does not see it,
The troubles from men are ceaseless,
At night they are worse;
He carries a bull gonorrhoea from the town
And smears it in my body,
We shall never have peace,
The pain is terrible,
At night it is worse.
I even bore him children,
My man bothers my head
With stupid words,
At night he is worse;
We women will never have peace,
We will never prosper, the troubles from men are ceaseless,
At night they are worse.[14]

ACHOLI (Uganda)

The poem is multi-thematic in as far as it talks about the man's despotism and insolence ("My man hurls insults at my mother"); alcoholism ("He drinks to his full"; infidelity ("He carries a bull gonorrhoea from the town"); and quarrelsomeness (My man bothers my head/with stupid words"). All these may be summarised as the man's irresponsibility. Yet thematically, the song could still be called a marriage song or a song about liberation or even a domestic song!

Using the thematic approach might also be limited by the fact that some oral poems may not have a theme to talk of. Such are the lullabies, catch rhymes, hide and seek games, play songs, e.t.c. Such limitations must be borne in mind when undertaking classification.

Functional Classification

This is classifying an oral poem according to its **didactic** or **artistic** purpose. What are the words of the poem supposed to convey? Is the poem supposed to praise, satirise, lament, encourage, indoctrinate or just entertain? Out of these purposes, we get such labels as: panegyric, satirical verse, lament, propaganda songs, hortatory poetry and elocutionary poetry. Below are two examples:

A Praise Poem

In Praise of the Ironsmith

Today this place is full of noise and jollity
The guiding spirit that enables my husband to forge makes him do wonders.
All those who lack hoes for weeding, come and buy!
Hoes and choppers are here in plenty.
My husband is a craftsman in iron,
Truly a wizard of forging hoes.
Ah, here they are! They have come eager to find hoes.
Ah, the iron itself is aglow, it is molten red with heat,
And the ore is ruddy and incandescent.
My husband is an expert in working iron
A craftsman who sticks like wax to his trade.
On the day when the urge to forge comes upon him,
The bellows do everything but speak.
The pile of slag rises higher and higher,
Just look at what has been forged,
At the choppers, at the hoes, at the battle axes,
And here at the pile of hatchets, large and small
Then look at the blood-bladed knives and the adzes.
Merely to list them all seems like boasting.
As for fowls and goats, they cover my yard.
They all come from the sale of tools and weapons.
Here is where you see me eating at ease with a spoon.[15]

SHONA (Zimbabwe)

100

A Satirical Verse

Lazybones, let's go to the farm
    Sorry, I've got a headache
Lazybones, let's go pounding
    Sorry, my leg isn't right
Lazybones, let's go fetch firewood
    Sorry, my hands are hurting
Lazybones, come and have some food
    Hold on, let me wash my hands.[16]

                                         CHI-TUMBUKA, (Malawi)

Contextual Criterion

The social context of a poem refers to the **where**, **when** and **circumstance** of a performance. As cultural expressions, oral art is rarely analysed independent of the social context as a background. The social context gives it an immediate application of meaning. From this approach of classifying poems, we get references such as: birth songs, circumcision songs, funeral songs, war songs, e.t.c. Here for example is a funeral song. It is part of the hour-long dirge chanted by the Yoruba poet Omobayode Arowa at the state funeral of Lieutenant Adekunle Fajuyi... Military Governor of Western Nigeria when he was killed... in July 1966. His state funeral was held in January 1967 . . .

In this dirge the former governor is mourned in terms appropriate to his position as a public figure... all suited to the expression of public loss. The closing lines present Fajuyi as a man distinguished in all his activities (at home, in the farm, in the palace, e.t.c. but in the end departing as a soldier 'on parade'.[17]

Dirge For Fajuyi

Dekunle, handsome man, hail!
And farewell!
It is goodbye, as when a stranger is seen off to the town gate,
Once dead and reborn, a person does not know the front of his father's house

Goodbye!
The stump of the palm tree does not owe a debt to the wind
Dekunle who lies dead here owed no personal obligation
Before he went to God
As a person walks, as on parade, so it is the soldier goes away,

O child of the big cloth, which makes the loom shake violently.
Greetings...

This is how people are,
That is how the end of things usually goes!
Look, the World is derisive
And the uninitiated man is happy;
The uninitiated man does not know that the World can mock one!
Make a display of tear-laden eyelids
And when a touraco cries it makes us feel like weeping.
The soldiers should have gone far;
Dekunle, I call you without stopping,
I call you, won't you please answer?
I call you five times, six times!
I call you seven times, eight times!
I call you sixteen times, where the Olubeje mushrooms grow abundantly and
    block the road!
I call you, won't you please answer?
It is all right then,
I am not angry,
It is all right then,
I, myself, am sad,
If you touch my face
        Tears, tears, tears!...

Greetings!
Fajuyi it has been a long time,
Fajuyi it has been a long time;
Your father calls you five times, six times!
He calls you seven times, eight times!
He calls you sixteen times,
Where the Olubeje mushrooms grow all over the road!
He calls you without stopping!
Your mother calls you too:
Do you hear anymore?
Your mother calls you without stopping
With tear-laden eyes,
As when the touraco cries!

It is all right then,
I am not annoyed,
There are days when things are like that!
O child of leopard.
Distinguished prince, it has been such a long time!
Child of the leopard at home,
Child of the leopard in the farm,
Child of the leopard, who wears a flower garment,
Child of the leopard, who has the Ogele dress,
Child of the leopard, clean from top to toe,
Child of the leopard, clean to the tip of his tail,
Child of the leopard, who walks freely in the palace,
Who will chain the leopard?
He is going in the sky
     An aeroplane!
As a person walks, as on parade,
So it is the soldier goes away.[18]

YORUBA (Nigeria)

Contextual classification is also very field work oriented. All the same, it is also true that certain poems may be performed in more than one occasion (context). For example, a poem celebrating a victory in a cattle raid may also be performed by the warriors during a beer party. In this context, it would be classified as a beer party song.

Because of this adaptability along many social contexts, such a classification depends on description of the actual details of the occasion.

Personal Criterion

In this system, the poem is considered against the **person** or **people** who perform it: children, adults, adolescents, elders, males, females, the married, the single, e.t.c. Thus we get classes such as women's songs, children's songs, e.t.c. Below is an example of a women's song from the Maasai:

A Woman's Song

A man went into a fit outside the village
Coming to the hearth with it
Calm down my husband
Crush not the firestones

For you are the one who told Namerai's brother
To go and spend at the young woman's house
And he is neither a child with whom I have shared the breast
Nor is he the first born of my co-wife
And you know the flesh of the petit-ribbed ones
Do not mind coming together

Lay down your fury old man
Let us load the donkey and move on
I have lauded Nampirdai with merry
Have done the same with Noolmong'i
Knowing that I am going to the high ground
Where he with the fluffy ostrich headdress lives
Where Ole Kaigil's headdress resides
The place where my flesh felt unsafe
The dapple spear, brother to Mosomba
Who wiped out the Kikuyus of Ndeiya[19]

MAASAI (Kenya)

The collector of this song, Naomy Kipury, explains that it is the kind of song performed during festivities when each woman takes time to express her intimate thoughts and experiences. In this particular song, the woman is taunting a jealous husband who told a young man to go and sleep in his wife's hut not knowing that the young man was already "a man".

Structural Criterion

The pattern of performance and number of performers is also a useful guideline to classification. Under this we can come up with **solo**, **choral** and **antiphonal** performances as categories.

In a solo performance, there is only one reciter, declaimer or singer. Lullabies are the best examples of solo performances but it is a pattern observable with even dirges, love songs, work songs, panegyrics e.t.c.

On the other hand, a choral performance involves a group voicing the words together in unison. This pattern is quite characteristic of children's play songs, religious creeds, circumcision songs, wedding songs e.t.c. There is for example the common choral chant the fans of a famous Kenyan football team, Gor Mahia, perform on their way from the stadium after a win. The chant goes:

Gor biro
Yawne yo
Gor biro
Yawne yo
Gor taya wang' ni meny ji duto
Gor taya wang' ni meny ji duto.

In translation it means:

Gor is coming
Clear for him the way
Gor is coming
Clear for him the way
Gor lantern this time shine on everyone
Gor lantern this time shine on everyone.

LUO (Kenya)

In the antiphonal, there is an alternation of at least two parties in the voicing of the words. Here is a good example of an antiphonal performance. It is the first part of a chant at the ancestral shrine by the Acholi of Uganda.

My clansmen I have called you to pacify this elephant

Elder: My clansmen, I have called you to pacify this elephant
As the elephant has come, let it come in peace.

All: It has come but let it come in peace.

Elder: There is a feud between you and us; you are our enemy
Your death will not be avenged.

All: It has come but let it come in peace.

Elder: As this has laid its head where others laid theirs
Let more others come.

All: Let them come, but come in peace.

Elder: You are our enemy, there is a feud between us,
You will die unavenged
Die peacefully;
Come in peace.

All: Come but come in peace.

Elder: I pray to the ancestors:
The Child has brought the head of an elephant home
As you used to do

ACHOLI (Uganda)

105

Although we have delineated the solo, antiphonal and choral patterns as distinct structural classes, it is important to note that many poems combine these structural elements in actual performance. A single performance can, for example, slide from the solo through the antiphonal to the choral or adapt any pattern infusing the three at different stages. This kind of characteristic again underscores the need to adopt a descriptive approach to classification.

Stylistic Criterion

The classification here would depend on the gradation of the performance according to the degree of departure from speech utterance. Thus we can talk of **recitation, declamation** and **song** as categories.

A recitation is a delivery marked by a pace faster than ordinary speech, maintained at an even rhythm and then a heightened pitch of voice. A declamation is a more developed recitation exhibiting characteristics of song without being definitely song. It is very eloquent and emotional. The classic example of declamation the author has come across is the Luo male's dirges. In moaning the dead, the Luo male does not wail as the female. He does what is called 'sigweya' or 'gweyo' meaning 'declamation'. He expresses himself in rapidly delivered words interspersed with interjections, exclamations and gestures portraying his sorrow. The pace is very fast but definitely not that of a song. Song then is the terminal degree of stylisation with a definite musical pace.

Having explored all these criteria, it is obvious that a comprehensive and exhaustive classification is no easy task. Each of the criteria gives us something about the performance but not all. We need to consider all of them to achieve a fuller classification. Thus we may come up with something like this to describe a poem: a recited (stylistic) solo (structure) female's (person) religious (content) thanksgiving (purpose/function) birth (context) poem. Quite a mouthful!

There are two ways out of the dilemma. First is to go for one or a combination of the criteria that is most relevant and applicable to the material. Second is to engage in the task of tabulating each poem against all the criteria and noting the relevant points on each. This can be done by having a detailed table listing all the aspects considered and the title of the poem. Let us use the following poem to illustrate.

Kĩrĩro: A Lament *by Wanjiru wa Kabuagara*

Gicui you came,
To greet Waceera (clan)
She came

She was drowned by a river
When it dried up the announcer died too

There is nothing I understand
When (you) our children come in and go out

Waceera, did you leave
That boy and Njeeri at home?

And I am an only child
Announcers when you reach Ceera (clan)
You greet Kigotho for me,
My father and I know he did not come.

O dear
Well
Ngewa, I have gone
Greet those of Njeeri (clan)
You hear, I told you
I am alone
I am the lone child of Wangari!
But now I am more able to wander
You hear?

I told you
I am all alone
I am the only child of Wangari
But now Waceera I am no more able to wander
You hear?

Oh dear
Well
Me of Njeeri I get milk
From my father Kigotho's cow
You hear?
And now stay in peace.[21]

GIKUYU (Kenya)

Classification Table Illustration

Poem	Traditional class	Subject	Function	Context	Performer	Structure	Style
Kiriro	For young People	Marriage	Lament	Wedding	Newly wed female	Solo	Song

STRUCTURE AND STYLE OF POETRY

Performance

What marks out oral from written poetry more than anything else is that element of performance-active expressing of the art. Poetry permeates various spheres of life which supply the social contexts. Thus we can in summary talk of:

Ceremonial poetry: those poems accompanying important community activities and rites e.g. birth, marriage, initiation, etc.

Vocational or Occupational poetry: to accompany chores like ploughing, weeding, harvesting, pounding, hunting, fishing, etc.

Socialisation or Leisure poetry: for entertainment e.g. play songs, wrestling songs, beer party songs, e.t.c.

The categorisation does not imply any uniformity in the performances of the poems falling under any one category. Actually, even the same poem by the same person is a different thing every other time it is performed.

In describing a performance, the following are important guidelines to consider:

1. Who performs – males, females, children, adults, elders?
2. Style of performance – song, declamation or recital?
3. Structure of performance – solo, choral or antiphonal?
4. Is there an audience? If so, how does the performer relate with it?
5. When is the performance i.e. during what ceremony, time of day, e.t.c. Is this restrictive or can the performance be done at other times and occasions?

6. What is the subject, tone and mood of the poem?
7. What is the purpose of the poem?
8. What accoutrements and musical instruments accompany the performance?

Taking the poetic genre as a whole the three patterns of performance – the solo, choral and antiphonal structures need highlighting.

Solo Performance

In this there is only one performer. It is characteristic of specific genres like lullabies, love songs and work songs where the chore is solitary. But there are also solo performances with regard to all other genres like panegyric, political poems, etc.

The success of a solo performance so much depends on the personal abilities of the performer. He must be very versatile in his use of language, drama, voice and the accompaniments at his disposal. He needs very effective personal qualities to appeal to and enthuse the audience.

Choral Performance

This is when a group performs simultaneously voicing the poem. Prior to the performance, there needs to be a session of practice to acquaint the choir with the words and patterns of the poem. The length of the practice depends on the length and complexity of the poem. With a simple straight forward poem a few minutes are enough to get the poem going e.g. with a repetitive ideophonic work song.

The most obvious advantage of the choral performance is the vocal power of projection. It also submerges the individual weaknesses and the end result is seen as a communal rather than an individual product.

On the other hand, the choral performance may suppress individual talent and actually personal weaknesses may mar what otherwise could be an excellent performance. As well, the individual may adapt a lethargic attitude towards perfecting the performance, believing that the inertia of the group would carry the day.

Antiphonal Performance or Strophe

Here there are two parties alternating in voicing the words. Most times there is a soloist calling the tune and a chorus answering. But this is not the rule as there are cases where the two parties are neither distinctly solo nor choral.

When there is a soloist, he is often an accomplished reciter or singer who has charisma and a powerful voice to motivate the chorus. He is the pivot of the performance and is stationed at a strategic position within the formation. In a linear formation, he is often in the front, while in the circular one he is mostly in the middle. Whatever the formation, the soloist exercises a lot of freedom of movement in relation with the other performers for effective conducting of the performance by maintaining a close contact with them.

As controller of the performance, he is also a decision-maker. He leads in choosing what is to be performed in what order. This factor is highly determined by the mood of the occasion and the group's repertoire. If the mood is warming up, the soloist is wise to follow with a more climatic poem rather than one which would dupe the audience's spirits. Even after deciding the poem, the soloist must also time it lest he under-reward the audience or likewise overstretches the poem.

In the course of an oral performance, there is a lot of variation both thematically and stylistically. The necessary changes are cued by the soloist by switching to the right code. This requires a very sharp and accurate mental coordination for a smooth and coherent transition.

Quite frequently, there is more than one soloist in a group performance. Each soloist may specialise on specific songs. Alternatively they may share in leading the songs at different points, alternating as the need may be.

Meanwhile the chorus offers the backup, dance and drama.

The antiphonal form has the credit of exploiting the talents of the soloist, not in isolation but as a member of the group. A soloist obviously has a superior vocal facility. Yet his success is not independent of the whole troupe. While acknowledging his centrality in the performance, we cannot fail to recognise the contribution of the chorus.

Another inherent advantage is that it creates variety both vocally and visually. The audience is not condemned to the drone and monotony of one person. And the group dwarfs individual weaknesses.

On the other hand, it has definite weaknesses. If the soloist is very powerful, he tends to domineer over the other performers and they may develop an over-dependence on him at the detriment of developing other talents. The soloist could also become complacent and presumptuous. And at the technical level, the strophe requires a lot of time for the perfection of patterns and vocal coordination.

Notwithstanding these weaknesses the strophe remains one of the most powerful and common forms of poetic performances in Africa.

Drama, Accoutrements and Instrument

The word 'drama' is used here in the sense of 'non-verbal' action that goes on in a performance. This may be quite limited or elaborate. In a lullaby, the drama includes the swaying and rocking of the child to and fro. And in the self-praise poem, there is a lot of

110

head-shaking, hand gestures and bodily movements in the arena. However passive or effusive the drama is, it enhances the mood and theme of the poem.

Much in line with the drama is the instrumental accompaniment and clothing especially in songs. Instruments heighten the mood and rhythm of the song and actually promote its reception. The same way, the attire, be it a headgear, skinwear etc., emphasises the gestures and therefore creates visual beauty. Here is a brief description of the drama involved in dirges to illustrate the point.

Okot p'Bitek says of Acholi dirges:

> The dirges of Acholi form an important part of the conventionalised and dramatised outburst of grief and wailing, with which the people face the supreme crisis of death.[22]

This is quite true of many communities where dirges are performed e.g. the Akan of Ghana, Luhyia and the Luo of Kenya. Among the Luo, dirges are performed by both men and women.

A woman singing a dirge performs some kind of involuntary dance plodding the compound where the corpse lies in state. She holds her waist or head in disbelief, hits her hands against the thighs, wipes tears from the eyes and blows phlegm from the nose while shrieking in tantrums that may also include rolling on the ground. At the end of it all, she is red-eyed, physically tired and with a husky voice.

The man can alternatively be heard voicing his dirge from afar as he approaches the funeral. He carries a huge club, blows a horn and wears a headgear. As he nears the homestead, the outburst becomes more dramatic as he breaks into short sprints spearing in the air in a mock fight with death.

Although the emphasis of dirges are in the words, the drama is so conspicuous it cannot be ignored.

Audience

Not all performers of poetry have an audience e.g. lullabies and children's play songs don't. But when an audience is there, it motivates the performer and a reciprocal relationship develops.

An audience can motivate and also demoralise a performer. One that claps and applauds the performer gives him confidence and makes him put up his best. Often the reactions go beyond just claps and cheers to actual joining in the performance to do a jig here and a twist there, a chorus here and a piece of material reward now and again in some communities like the Luo Nyatiti player who is showered with coins as he plays his lyre.

Both the performer and the audience derive some utility out of the occasion and each plays its appropriate role to realise that goal.

Structure

The anatomy of a narrative is more or less fixed to; introduction, conflict, crisis, climax and denouement. Not so with poetry. Each poem has its own unique plot and therefore pattern of development – structure.

First attention to the structure of a poem goes to the verses and stanzaic arrangement. Is the poem mono-stanzaic or multi-stanzaic? This question is not very easy to answer with oral poetry since the whole layout depends on the transcriber of the poem. The second consideration is whether the poem is antiphonal or not.

After these, concern is with a keener examination of the rationale for the arrangement. Mono-stanzaism could be a result of the unity of theme or continuity of performance while multi-stanzaism may be due to diversity in theme and pauses or breaks in the performance. Where there is antiphony, the relationship between the lead and supporting verses should be established. In typical antiphony, the solo parts vary while the chorus parts are repetitive. But any exception must be treated on its own merit.

Structural variation in poetry arises from the shift in theme, mood and voices. A poem may glide from the mundane to the abstract, a light to heavy mood, a character to another. As this happens, a certain unity of development is maintained. How do the words, images and ideas relate? Are they random or carefully chosen?

Repetition and parallelism are two important aspects of structure. Repetition can be of sound, word, line, idea, e.t.c. at regular or random intervals. What purposes does it serve in the poem? Parallelism, the balancing of parts in a poem, occurs with words, sounds, lines, moods and ideas. It is an aspect mainly for the purpose of comparison and contrast. To grasp the point better, let us analyse them in the following poem.

My Journey to the Forest by Wanjiru wa Kabuagara.

My time to go to the forest had come
It was the whites and the homeguards
who prevented me.

One small white man asked a question
One bad question
This was the question,
Where did the black people come from?

112

One black man asked a question
One good question
And this was the question,
Where did the whites come from?

Homeguards will cry at noon
When you find you are neither in the skin nor in the flesh.[23]

GIKUYU

There is a structural repetition in stanza two and three. The lines correspond exactly, retaining the same word order e.g. 'one black man asked a question' is a structural repetition of the first line of stanza two.

And that overlaps and constitutes the first aspect of parallelism in the poem. Stanzaic parallelism is seen in the hemming in of the middle stanzas which are structurally similar, with the first and fourth displaying varying patterns from the two. The first stanza in this case acts as an introduction to the subject of resistance to colonialism by the singer taking off as a guerilla to the forest. The second and third stanzas focus on the crux of the matter—racism. And the last makes a conclusive remark warning the homeguards that their position in the struggle is precarious, ambivalent and unfruitful. So the parallelism lies in the comparison of stanzas two and three and the contrast of those with the other two.

There is also characterological and attitudinal parallelism. The question in the second stanza is asked by a white man while the one in the third is by a black man. The former asks a 'bad question' and the latter a 'good question'. In the phrases are revealed the singer's attitude. The singer is in obvious favour of the black man. Again we see that the second and third stanzas are rhetorical while the other two are declarative.

The brief illustration makes the idea of parallelism clear but it occurs in a variety of other ways in different poems.

Style

In this section, we look at the most important aspect of style associated with poetry. The system used is to see them in specific poems rather than discussing in a vacuum.

Imagery is the backbone of poetry. It achieves vivid configuration of the subject matter in the audience's mind. There are several aspects in imagery: simile, metaphor, personification, symbolism and hyperbole. Let us see them in the poem that follows.

The Timi of Ede
Huge fellow whose body fills an ant hill,
You are heavily pregnant with war

113

All your body except your teeth is black.

No one can prevent the ape
from sitting on the branch of a tree.

No one can dispute the throne with you.
No one can try to fight you.
One who shakes a tree trunk shakes himself.
We do not try to resist you
The seeds of the Ayo game
do not complain of being shoved about.
You are like death,
who plucks a man's eyeballs suddenly.
You are like a big ripe fruit
that falls on a child at midnight.

Fighting a battle in front
you mark out the next battlefield behind.
My lord, please give the world some rest.
If one greets you there is trouble;
if one does not greet you there is also trouble.
The fire of destruction is part of your baggage
whenever you go.
You kill your opponents gently,
like cutting a calabash in two.
When the leopard kills,
its tail trails gently on the ground.
Whenever you open your mouth wide,
you swallow a hero.[24]

YORUBA (Nigeria)

The Timi is described in a series of metaphors. He is said to be 'pregnant with war' to indicate his belligerence and the ability to unleash war any time. He is also seen as the 'ape ... sitting on the branch of a tree' to insinuate that he is natural to the throne as the ape is to its habitat. He is the unshakable tree trunk and the 'leopard'. The first image shows the permanence of his power and the second his ferocious ambivalence i.e. the tail trailing the ground gently. His subjects also refer to themselves in metaphoric terms. They are the 'seeds of the Ayo game' who 'do not complain of being shoved about'. That is, they are completely subservient to him.

114

There are also a number of similes in the poem. The Timi is 'like death' and 'like a big ripe fruit', both images meant to portray his elusiveness and unpredictability. His efficiency at killing is 'like cutting a calabash in two'.

The picture of the Timi is overblown and hence there is hyperbole in the poem. He is said to be so huge that his body fills an ant hill and also so black that only his teeth are white. That is a conceptual exaggeration. He is painted as being ubiquitous in the words:

> Fighting a battle in front
> you mark out the next battlefield behind.

Meanwhile he is humorously and metaphorically shown as an undoer of heroes, nominally, their swallower. All these exaggerations tell us about the awe in which the singer holds the Timi.

We do not fail to recognise the idiomatic expressions:

> No one can prevent the ape
> from sitting on the branch of a tree.

and

> One who shakes a tree trunk shakes himself.

Without overstretching the beauty of that poem, let us illustrate personification and symbolism in the next poem.

Hymn to the Sun

> The fearful night sinks
> trembling into the depths
> before your lightning eye
> and the rapid arrows
> from your fiery quiver.
> With sparkling blows of light
> you tear her cloak
> the black cloak lined with fire
> and studded with gleaming stars –
> with sparkling blows of light
> you tear the black cloak.[25]

FANG

In this poem the sun is seen as a warrior with quivers shooting and perforating darkness. The darkness is called 'her' and so the sun, by imputation is 'he'. In both cases, the phenomena are personified. In fact one can sense a sexual undertone in the whole poem.

115

The sun tears the black cloak of darkness, in much the same way as a rapist does to his victim.

The speaker in the poem sees the sun as a conqueror. To him dawn is a victory, a symbol of triumph. It can be easily guessed that the Fang regard the sun as a powerful sign of triumph, and pride.

Let us now look at 'persona' and 'allegory'. 'Persona' means the person in whose point of view the poem is presented. Allegory is basically the fact of having a story within a story. The next poem exhibits both.

The Train

The train
carries everybody
everywhere.

It carries the men
It carries the women
It carries me too
a blind boy,
wherever it carries me
alas I meet distress
and knock against it
with my knee.
It carries the men
it carries the women,
It carries the blind boy
to his distress.[26]

ITESO

The persona in this poem is the blind boy. He talks of a train journey in rather melancholic terms, as a vehicle to doom. But beneath the story of the train journey, the idea really is that of life. The train is carrying 'everybody/everywhere'. It is not a physical train. It is life. And life has a whole mix of people – men, women, the blind, the seeing, e.t.c. Its milieu is a muddle that is as uncomfortable as the train journey to the blind boy. This story within the story of the poem makes it an allegory.

Finally the next poem is used to illustrate: irony, sarcasm, satire, allusion and rhetoric.

Father Holy Truecross

Every man born of woman
lives in his land, his home.

116

Only poor exiles
have neither land nor home.
Father Holy Truecross
You say that I am your son.
But if you have no penis
How are you going to father me?
Father Holy Truecross,
You say that I am lazy,
But you are more lazy than I
You are asleep to what is going on
Father Holy Truecross
I greet you 'good day'
But because you haven't responded
I knock you to the ground with the pigs.[27]

QUECHEA (Bolivia)

The irony in this poem is in the name 'Father Holy Truecross'. The speaker thinks of fatherhood in the biological sense. And if the father is celibate, then how can he be a biological father? This criticism is brought out in the rhetorical lines:

But if you have no penis
How are you going to father me?

In the same lines is inlaid the sarcasm. The lines are meant to hurt the pride of the father by questioning his virility. The whole poem is a bitter challenge to the credibility of the father. He is seen as some kind of a fugitive, sexually dead, lazy and ignorant.

The poem makes several allusions. Father's penislessness is an allusion to the institution of celibacy. The name 'Father' is of course the designation of priesthood while the cross is the insignia of the Christian faith.

The poem satirises the priest and poses the questions about his holiness. It is a protest song to resist Spanish missionary attempts to impose their religion on the Bolivians. The singer sees them as fugitives with noble backgrounds and therefore who cannot stay in their homes and lands. And they think they are in control of the situation while actually they are so ignorant of the people's machinations against them.

These are not the only stylistic aspects of poetry but a representative lot. The mnemonic devices – alliteration, assonance, ideophone and rhime are explained in chapter one.

117

SOCIAL FUNCTIONS OF POETRY

Poetry, whether recited, declaimed or sung, has got certain ends to meet. It is these ends that we call social functions. They could be very mundane or very philosophical and abstract. In this text, we have divided the functions into:

(a) Socialisation
(b) Aesthetics
(c) Interfluence
(d) Social commentary
(e) Cultural and Historical record

Socialisation

Socialisation can be understood in two ways: as a way of fitting one into a social fabric or as a way of deriving pleasure through entertainment. The sense in which poetry is a socialiser encompasses both the cases as we obviously derive pleasure from poetry, since it is an art, but also derive some information intended to cultivate in us the sense of the social fabric from which the poetry is created.

To illustrate, let us take the occasion of a children's play song from the Luo. In this particular play song, the children sing as they pass under a bridge of arms formed by their leaders. At the end of each cycle of the song, a player is held and asked to name his or her preferences of food. If it is a vegetable, the player lines behind the leader whose trademark is the vegetable and if it is a carcass, the player lines behind the other leader. At the end when all players have got sides, there is a tug of war.

This occasion socialises in several ways. There is a division of labour and recognition of leadership hence there is an element of organisation among the players. The social organisation is ensured by the rules of play (i.e. having to go through the bridge, be held, name ones preference, line up and then pull for ones side in the tug of war). The player is conditioned to accept the rules and more so to accept that anybody could join his or her group by virtue of choosing the type of food preferred. This is because the players do not know what each leader has chosen and each has to whisper the choice when held at the bridge. Then the vigour of movement, dance and pulling becomes an interactive process which is also a vent for pent-up energies and creation of pleasure.

Of course the pleasure derived from a poetic performance is for both the audience and the players as well whether it emanates from the play on words, movement and dance, attire, humour and so on. A bit of humour in this short woman's pounding song:

Eyes of Hunger

You made me marry a man with a bald head
You could spread flour on it to dry
If you put a penny on it, it falls down;
Eyes of hunger, e-e
You made me marry a man with a bald head.[28]

CHISENA (Malawi)

Aesthetics

To qualify to be performed, there must be something of beauty in a poem. This beauty lies in the language. Out of the linguistic resources, poetry selects what is most appealing and puts it together.

The aspect of play on sounds comes out so powerfully in the ideophones, alliteration, assonance, rhime and rhythm. As well, there are the poems in which the words are not expressly meant for semantic communication but more as artistic expressions. This is the category of poems called elocutionary. The best examples are chain songs. Even under the elocutionary poems there are some poems with very philosophical foundations. Such are the Gikuyu Gĩcandĩ from Kenya. Gĩcandĩ is basically a proverbial contest between two elder men in poetry. It involves the coding and decoding of messages that are always given in proverbs. If a singer fails to decode a message from his opponent, he hands over his gourd (gĩcandĩ) to the winner. The winner takes the loser's Gĩcandĩ with him never to return it unless the losing composer wins it back in the same way he lost it.[29]

The contest is a very beautiful and challenging exercise where people test their wits and mastery of the resources of their language through a spontaneous delivery. It is an occasion for bringing to the fore the aesthetic qualities of the language stock.

The pith of poetic aesthetics is in the imagery. Powerful imagery is the sauce of good poetry and it attains better communication than prosaic language. Let us take an example of a poem that uses a lot of images.

Death has Crushed my Heart

My brother's death has crushed my heart.
My brother has left me at crossroads
My brother has left me hanging over the fire like a
parcel of meat to dry
But a parcel of meat over the fire will still have
somebody to touch it.

119

Death has turned me up like cocoyam and peeled
off my tubers
My left hand has turned to my back
Death has turned me into bitterness itself
My mirror is broken
My own is past.[30]

IGBO (Nigeria)

In this poem, someone mourns a dead brother. The mourner laments the death of the brother who has been his benefactor. He is left lonely and helpless without the brother.

The poem is outstanding in the use of imagery. In the line 'death has crushed my heart', the mourner establishes a metaphor depicting death as a huge boulder that has suddenly landed on his lifeline causing total destruction. The image of the heart symbolises the centre of life. The dead brother was the centre of his life.

The mourner is thus in a dilemma and has no sense of direction as portrayed in the line 'my brother has left me at crossroads'. He has been left in a precarious and uncertain position: 'hanging over the fire like a parcel of meat to dry'. By stating that the meat has 'someone to touch it' the mourner emphasies the hopelessness of his position. He is left orphan-like and unprotected. He is like a reaped cocoyam whose peels have been ripped off. The death has not only separated him from the brother, but also denied him protection. Death here has in fact been personified.

We are further shown the man's dilapidation in the idiomatic expressions 'My left hand has turned to my back' and 'My own is past'. The first means that his strength is broken; he is left as the weaker left hand, his dead brother having been the stronger right hand. 'My own past' implies that he is completely doomed.

Despite being a dirge, the beauty of the imagery in that poem is not lost to us.

Interfluence

This is the coming together of two or more genres in one performance. Poetry especially augments narratives. The case has been analysed in detail under the 'Structure and Style' of narratives.

Social Commentary

We defined poetry as the powerful expression of human feelings, thought and ideas in language. Two broad categories may be identified: Socio-functional and aesthetic poetry. In the former, there is pre-occupation with the divulgence of messages and in the latter it is with the beauty of artistic expression. In this section, our concern is with the former.

Human feelings range from the extremes of exuberance to dejection and melancholy depending on the experiences behind them. In poetry, people express their feelings and ideas about life whether it is a fulfilling or discouraging experience. Let us exemplify with this lullaby:

Lullaby

Someone would like to have you for her child
but you are mine.
Someone would like to rear you on a costly mat
but you are mine.
Someone would like to place you on a camel blanket
but you are mine.
I have you to rear on a torn old mat.
Someone would like to have you for her child
but you are mine.[31]

AKAN (Ghana)

In this lullaby, a mother expresses her ownership of the child. She makes very important though indirect comments about the nature of life in the lullaby. She has no inferior feelings about her poverty and is proud to nurse her baby on the old and torn mat. The 'someone' who would like to own the child is impliedly childless. The comment here is that nature does not deny one everything. In terms of African thought and philosophy, the poor mother is even better placed than the affluent one because she is fertile and is therefore "a complete woman".

Even in as grim poems as dirges we get poignant points about social life. The example of Acholi dirges is quite handy. In some of these dirges, there are satirical comments about institutions of life. Here is an example on leviratic marriage unions.

He has Left his Wealth to the Inheritor

He has left all his wealth to the inheritor, oh;
He, the beautiful son of Amoo
left all his wealth;
He left all the cattle to the inheritor,
Now the inheritor boasts with them;
He left all his wealth, I am sad;
The man left all his wealth, to others,
What a lucky inheritor!

He left his iron-roofed house to the inheritor,
Ee, the son of Amoo was most generous;

He left his bicycle to the inheritor, oh,
This man boasts for nothing,
He got all the wealth from the dead
He left all his wealth for the inheritor,
Ha, this inheritor is most lucky.[32]

ACHOLI (Uganda)

While mourning the dead, this poem concentrates on deriding the inheritor who has been left many things he could not have got on his own. The comment being made is that those who inherit widows somewhat stand to gain economically. So death to them is a welcome occurrence in a way.

Poetry in all other forms is a vehicle of social comment on different aspects of life as the two foregoing poems show.

Cultural and Historical Record

Since poetry is composed out of experience, history is recorded in it. Certain genres like war songs, praise poems of kings and heroic poems particularly abound in historical allusions about people, events and places. One of the best examples of historical events recorded in poetry is the struggle against colonialism. The song below is an example from Kenya.

Those who Sold their People

We agreed to carry this log
together and when we reached the middle of the river
Those who ran away and sold their people
And burst our houses
Now their children are like those of Goliath.

Now Mumbi is in hospital
Let's pray that Gikuyu will have a good issue
Let her get a boy who we shall call Freedom,
And if she gets a girl, we shall name her 'Our Land!'

Let us praise those of us in Nyandarua forest.
Dedan Kimathi and General Mathenge, General Kago and
General Waruingi.

122

Our people have you forgotten
The Gikuyu proverb that
One cannot eat what he has not sweated for.[33]

GIKUYU (Kenya)

The historical event in the poem is that while the patriots went to the forest to fight, the loyalists reaped the colonial benefits. Then when independence came, it is the latter who found themselves in commanding social positions having alienated the land and imbibed western education. It is a fact of life that the children of the colonial chiefs went to school and became socio-economic heavyweights (Goliaths) in the post-independence era.

The poem gives us the names of fighters in Nyandarua forest and therefore acts as a historical document.

It seems to have been composed on the verge of independence or soon after. The idea of Mumbi 'in hospital' symbolises expectation of independence, and the names Mumbi and Gikuyu allude to the mythical progenitors of the Gikuyu community – another aspect of historical documentation.

Then we are told that the child would be named 'Freedom' or 'Our Land'. This takes us to the tradition of naming people in the group. Without doubt we can say that the Gikuyu name after historical events as is the case with many other African peoples.

Going out of East Africa we can exemplify cultural reflections from the Yoruba religious poems, like the longish one below that talks about the 'Ori', one of the divinities in Yoruba traditional religion.

The Importance of Ori

Orunmila said that one always bends down when entering the doorway.
Ifa asked the question, 'Who among you Gods could follow your
        devotee to a distant journey over the seas?'
Sango answered that he could follow his devotee to a distant journey
        over the seas.
The question was asked from him, 'What will you do if after
        travelling for a long distance,
Walking and walking,
You arrive at Koso,
The home of your fathers?
If they prepare Gbegiri soup,
And they prepare yam-flour pudding;
If they offer you bitter kola

123

And a cock?
Sango answered, 'After eating to my satisfaction,
I will return home'.
Sango was told that he could not follow his devotee to a distant
    journey over the seas.
Orunmila said that one always bends down when entering the doorway.
Ifa asked the question, 'Who among you Gods could follow your
    devotee to a distant journey over the seas?'
Oya answered that she could follow her devotee to a distant
    journey over the seas.
The question was asked from her, 'What will you do if after
    travelling for a long distance,
Walking and walking,
You arrive at the city of Ira,
The home of your fathers?
If they kill a big animal,
And they offer you a big pot of egbo?'
Oya answered, 'After eating to my satisfaction,
I will return home'.
Oya was told that she could not follow her devotee to a distant
    journey over the seas.
Orunmila said that one always bends down when entering the doorway.
Ifa asked the question, 'Who among you Gods could follow your
    devotee to a distant journey over the seas?'
Oosala answered that he could follow his devotee to a distant
    journey over the seas.
The question was asked from him, 'What will you do if after
    travelling for a long distance,
Walking and walking,
You arrive at the city of Ifon,
The home of your fathers?
If they kill for you one big hen pregnant with eggs:
If they offer you two hundred snails
Seasoned with vegetables and melon soup?'
Oosala answered saying, 'After eating to my satisfaction,
I will return to my home'.

Oosala was told that he could not follow his devotee to a distant
    journey over the seas.
Orunmila said that one always bends down when entering the doorway.
Ifa asked the question, 'Who among you Gods could follow your
    devotee to a distant journey over the seas?'
Elegbara answered that he could follow his devotee to a distant
    journey over the seas.
The question was asked from him, 'What will you do if after
    travelling for a long distance,
Walking and walking,
You arrive at the city of Ketu,
The home of your fathers?
If they offer you a cock
And plenty of palm-oil?'
Elegbara answered, 'After eating to my satisfaction,
I will return home'.
Elegbara was told that he could not follow his devotee to a distant
    journey over the seas.
Orunmila said that one always bends down when entering the doorway.
Ifa asked the question, 'Who among you Gods could follow your
    devotee to a distant journey over the seas?'
Ogun answered that he could follow his devotee to a distant
    journey over the seas.
The question was asked from him, 'What will you do if after
    travelling for a long distance,
Walking and walking,
You arrive at Ire,
The home of your fathers?
If they offer you fried beans,
And they kill a dog for you
Together with a hen:
If they offer you guinea-corn beer and palm-wine?'
Ogun answered saying, 'After eating to my satisfaction,
I will chant, Ijala loudly and joyously
Back to my home'.
Ogun was told that he could not follow his devotee to a distant
    journey over the seas.

Orunmila said that one always bends down when entering the doorway.
Ifa asked the question 'Who among you Gods could follow your
    devotee to a distant journey over the seas?'
Osun answered that she could follow her devotee to a distant
    journey over the seas.
The question was asked from her, 'What will you do if after
    travelling a long distance,
Walking and walking,
You arrive at Ijumu,
The home of your fathers?
If they give you plenty of corn-starch pudding
Together with yanrin vegetable and maize beer?'
I will ride upon small pieces of brass back to my home'.
Osun was told that she could not follow her devotee to a distant
    journey over the seas.
Orunmila said that one always bends when entering the doorway
Ifa asked the question, 'Who among you Gods could follow your
    devotee to a distant journey over the seas?'
Orunmila said that he could follow his devotee to a distant
    journey over the seas.
The question was asked from him, 'What will you do if after
    travelling for a long distance,
Walking and walking,
You arrive at Igeti hill,
The home of your fathers?
If they offer you two fast-moving rats,
Two fish that swim gracefully,
Ten hens with big livers,
Two goats heavy with foetus,
Two cows with fat horns,
And they prepare yam flour-pudding:
If you take well-brewed guinea-corn beer,
And you take alligator pepper,
And good kola nuts?'
Orunmila answered saying, 'After eating to my satisfaction,
I will return to my home'

126

Orunmila was told that he could not follow his devotee to a distant
    journey over the seas.
Ifa priest was dumbfounded.
He could not say a word.
Because he didn't understand the parable.
Orunmila I confess my helplessness:
Please clothe me with wisdom,
Mapo in the city of Elere,
Mokun of the town of Otan,
Mesin of the city of Ilawe,
Mapo in the city of Elejelu:
Gbolajokoo, offspring of tusks
That make the elephant trumpet.
Orunmila you are the leader,'
I am the follower.
You are the sage who teaches one wise things like one's relation.
Ifa the question is, 'Who among the Gods can follow his devotee
    to a distant journey over the seas?'
Ifa said, 'It is Ori,
It is Ori alone
Who can follow his own devotee to a distant journey over the seas'.
Orunmila said, 'When an Ifa priest dies,
People may ask that his divination instruments should be thrown
    into the ditch.
When a devotee of Sango dies,
People may ask that his Sango instruments should be thrown away with him'
When a devotee of Oosala dies,
People may ask that his paraphernalia should be buried with him'
Orunmila asked, 'Ever since human beings have been dying,
Whose head is ever severed from his body before burial?
Ifa said, 'it is Ori
It is Ori alone
Who can follow his own devotee to a distant journey over the seas
    without turning back'.
If I have money
It is Ori whom I will praise.

127

My Ori, it is you
It is Ori whom I will praise.
My Ori it is you.
All the good things I have on earth,
It is my Ori to whom I will give praise.
My Ori it is you.
Ori I hail you,
You who always remembers your devotee,
You who give blessing to your devotee more quickly than
        other gods.
No God blesses a man
Without the consent of his Ori
Ori I hail you,
You who allows children to be born alive.
A person whose sacrifice is accepted by his own Ori
Should rejoice exceedingly.[34]

YORUBA (Nigeria)

The poem gives a succinct summary of Yoruba polytheism. The gods mentioned perform the functions bracketed as follows: Sango (god of thunder; the boldest god); Oya (the wife of Sango); Oosala (creation god); Elegbara (trickster god); Ogun (god of iron); Osun (gentle god of children and nursing mothers); and Orunmila (leader of the gods). Noting on the poem, Mapanje and Landig quote W. Abimbola:

> Ori is regarded as an intermediary between every man and the divinity whom he worships. Each individual's Ori is his personal divinity who regulates his life in conformity with the wisdom of the divinities who exist for the general public interest. Whatever has been sanctioned by ones Ori cannot be done by the divinities. Ori is the most important part of each individual's personality... The point of this story (in the poem) is to demonstrate the importance of Ori in the life of every individual. The Yoruba conceive of Ori as each individual's own guardian and divinity. The other Orisa are for the public at large. Although they cater for the interests of individuals, they cannot do this as effectively as Ori whose duty it is to protect the individual and lead him to his chosen destiny.[35]

From a people's poems we also get hints about their economic activities. Thus in a pastoralist group we get frequent references to cattle and their products. Quoting from the Akan, there is a poem about the hunters and the results of their trade.

128

Is the Chief Greater than the Hunter?

Is the chief greater than the hunter?
    Arrogance! Hunter? Arrogance!
The pair of beautiful things on your feet,
The sandals that you wear,
How did it happen?
It is the hunter that killed the duiker;
The sandals are made of skin of the duiker.

Does the chief say he is greater than the hunter?
    Arrogance! Hunter? Arrogance!
The noisy train that leads you away,
The drum that precedes you,
The hunter killed the elephant,
The drum head is the ear of the elephant;
Does the chief say he is greater than the hunter?
    Arrogance! Hunter? Arrogance.[36]

AKAN (Ghana)

A warning needs however to be sounded on the value of poetry as records of culture and history lest we think that it is a substitute for the two. Poetry is essentially art and art does not operate in the same way as History or Anthropology. The following can be regarded as the differential points:

- A poem does not strictly record the dates of the events and their chronology.
- It is difficult to sketch the exact events behind a poem from the independent poem. Poems are mainly commentaries on events. Thus we need to rely on other records for a historically accurate account. This underscores the need for a multi-disciplinary approach to the study of Orature.
- History concerns itself with elaborate details about causation and effects. Poems only siphon the emotive elements e.g. triumph or defeat for expression in song. Therefore the poems leave large gaps in the historical plot and deliberately distort facts to suit the purposes of the community.

Okot aptly summarises the point in this small account, which is an appropriate conclusion to this section.

In 1916 there was a fierce famine in East Acholi. The people of Pajule migrated to the western part of the country to seek succour. There was plenty of sweet potatoes in that area, and many lives were saved. When the famine was over the chief of Pajule came to persuade his people to return home. A poet replied with this song:

First you go and fetch
Those entombed in the stomach of hyenas,
And those who perished in the river,
And then show us the millet granaries;
Then we shall return to the east;
Where are the millet granaries?

The song is historical but only in a special way. It is silent on a number of questions that an ordinary historian would ask. What was the cause of the famine? Did the entire Pajule people migrate to the west? Among which people did they stay? How many people perished in the famine? And so on.[37]

From all these accounts, we do appreciate that poems reflect facets of a people's life, what they practise and believe in and what has so far shaped their way of life.

NOTES

1. Ruth Finnegan, *Oral Literature in Africa*, Oxford University Press: Nairobi, 1970, P. 87.
2. Ibid. p. 88.
3. Ibid. p. 89.
4. Ibid. p. 91.
5. Ibid. p. 201-2.
6. Okot p'Bitek, *Horn of my Love*, Heinemann: Nairobi, 1974, p. 4.
7. Ibid. p. 13.
8. Ibid. p. 168.
9. Ibid.
10. Ibid. p. 170
11. Finnegan. op.cit. p. 269-270.
12. p'Bitek, op.cit. p. 9.
13. Naomi Kipury, *Oral Literature of the Maasai*, Heinemann: Nairobi, 1983, p. 221-2.
14. p'Bitek, op.cit. p. 9.
15. Jack Mapanje and Landeg White, *Oral Poetry in Africa*, Longman: New York, 1983, p. 15.
16. Ibid. p. 93.
17. Ibid. p. 199.
18. Ibid. p. 182.
19. Kipury, op.cit. p. 217.
20. p'Bitek, op.cit. p.96. What is presented in this text is an edited version of the original poem.
21. Wanjiku Mukabi Kabira and Karega Mutahi, *Gikuyu Oral Literature*, Heinemann: Nairobi, 1988, p. 161-2.

22. p'Bitek, op.cit. p. 21.
23. Kabira and Mutahi, op.cit. p. 156.
24. Ulli Beier, *African Poetry*, Cambridge University Press: 1966, p. 42-3.
25. Ibid. p. 22.
26. Ibid. p. 35.
27. S. Kichamu Akivaga and A. B. Odaga, *Oral Literature: A School Certificate Course*, Heinemann: Nairobi, 1982, p. 88.
28. Mapanje and White, op.cit. p. 93.
29. Kabira and Mutahi, op.cit. p. 28.
30. Romanus Egudu and Donatus Nwoga, *Igbo Traditional Verse*, Heinemann: London, 1973, p. 74.
31. Beier, op.cit. p. 63.
32. p'Bitek, op.cit. p. 142.
33. Kabira and Mutahi, op.cit. p. 157.
34. Mapanje and White, op.cit. p. 124-8.
35. Ibid. p. 204.
36. Ibid. p. 61-2.
37. p'Bitek, op.cit. p. 156.

PART FOUR
NARRATIVES

"The continent has it own fictive traditions; it has the tradition of story, narrated orally... the medium through which Africa down the centuries has bared its soul, taught its (people) and entertained itself."

B. Onyango Ogutu and A. A. Roscoe, *Keep My words*, Heinemann: Nairobi, 1974.

What is a Narrative?

A narrative is basically a prose account of people, events, places, e.t.c. that may be factual or fictional. The accounts are principally handed down from person to person and generation to generation through word of mouth. The terms "tale" and "folktale" have been used to denote the same concept.

THEORIES OF ORAL NARRATIVES

The oral narrative is perhaps the most extensively collected and studied genre in oral literature. Before delving into an analysis of this genre, the text looks at the major theories which underlie the study of the genre.

One such theory is **evolutionism** which proposes that oral literature is a reflection of previous existence from which it has evolved. Evolutionism contends that the nature of man is basically the same universally and that all human societies develop similar traits even if they are geographically separate. The standpoint of evolutionism is that "certain psychic universals or elementary ideas uniting all cultures at identical stages of development" make it possible that "given a similar state of taste and fancy, similar beliefs... circumstances, a similar tale might conceivably be independently evolved in regions removed from each other". The theory is divided into **euhemerism**, **solarism** and **naturalism**.

According to euhemerism, one sub-theory of evolutionism, primitive man was unable to comprehend the nature of divinity and therefore resorted to belief in many gods with deities as his focus of awe, admiration, e.t.c. According to David Hume, primitive societies derived their deities by deifying societal heroes whom they looked upon as sources of powerful sensation. In a nutshell, the euhemerists hold that "all tales, especially of the heroic kind, primarily have to do with antecedent historical personalities and their experiences".

Solarism, a theory propounded by Max Muller, Jacom Grimm and Wilheim Grimm in the 19th Century saw the sun as the principal force behind all tales. Muller reached this conclusion when he studied Aryan mythology and found out that the tales degenerated into fragments as the Aryan people migrated westwards to Europe. But the solaristic model was invalidated as soon as James Frazer revealed in *The Golden Bough* that the solar deities such as the Egyptian Osiris first had an agrarian existence before being deified as solar deities. Frazer's theory led back to naturalism.

The evolutionist theories take the viewpoint that all societies progress from primitivity towards Europe-like civilisation. They state simply that a people's oral literature is created through some diffuse collective authorship. This view is summarised in the words of Henri Junod.

...tales are not created, on all sides by individual authors, but they are modified, altered and enriched as they are transmitted from one person to another, ... one race to another, to such an extent that new types, ... combinations, are adapted and a true development takes place.

It may appear that this approach simplifies the authorship of oral narratives. The claim of collective ownership is made without an explicit explanation being given as to how this takes place in the creation of a totally new narrative. It seems to be a convenient escape into the acknowledgement that tracing the historical origins of the tale is a convoluted affair, if not an impossible one.

Ruth Finnegan, in *Oral Literature in Africa* disagrees with evolutionists and observes that they devalue the role of the performer who is, in her view, the narrative maker. "The verbal elaboration, the drama of the performance itself, everything in fact, which makes it a truly aesthetic product", she says, "comes from the contemporary teller and his audience and not the remote past".

Evolutionism underlies the study of oral literature as a past rather than a present subject. It implies that authenticity lies with the past and that the further into remoteness one goes, the nearer he will be getting to the essential narrative. The obsession with the past of origins is severely limited by the fact that society is in constant transition and is therefore always primitive in retrospect.

The second theory, **diffusionism**, also called the Historical-Geographical Theory, emphasises the relationship between and among narratives from different societies with the aim of proving that there must have been some contact between the peoples historically or geographically. It negates the concept that similar tales could have emanated from different societies without that contact. The diffusionist explanation for the variations in what appears to be one tale from different societies is that the host community assimilated the tale by infusing their own to fit the tale into their cultural milieu.

The theory is associated with Theodor Benfey, Emmanuel Cosquin and Julius and Kearle Krohn. Benfey claims that Indian tales spread to the west through Islam. Cosquin, on the other hand, followed the Indianist theory but believed that the Indian tales could have originated in Egypt since Egyptian civilisation is older than the Indian. Meanwhile, the Krohns sought to establish the motifs in Finnish songs whose geographical distribution they traced in order to derive what variations may have been undergone in the process of passing on from one place to another. The work of Kearle and his student Anttii Aarne was later adapted and translated by Stith Thompson as *The Types of Folktales and Motif Index of Folk Literature*.

Embedded in diffusionism is the belief that an archetype tale must have existed in the community before its variations were adapted by other communities. In the section on classification, we look at some of the motifs, or recurrent patterns identifiable among Luo, Maasai and Gikuyu narratives. While evolutionists would attribute the similarity to universals shared by all communities, diffusionists would want to trace which of the communities it existed in first and to establish that the community had contact with the others.

Following this parameter, it is possible to conclude that if a tale is recorded to have existed in one society before it was observed in another, then the first society had it first and the second must have received it from the first.

For instance, there is a Luo narrative about a legendary hero called Luanda Magere. The narrative very closely resembles the biblical Samson and Delilah story. A diffusionist would probably argue that the Luo narrative must have been adapted from the biblical story and support the argument by citing the advent of colonialism in Africa and hence the introduction of Christian legends into the Luo community. Whether that is empirically defensible is a question for inquiry.

Diffusion, like evolutionism, does not focus on the creative aspects of oral narratives but concentrates on a mechanical classification process, looking at society as monolithic and not the metropolis it is becoming increasingly. The metropolitan trend has led to situations where certain corpus of oral literature appear universal and may not be attributable to any particular community of origin. How then is the archetype or the origin of the tale to be determined? Stith Thompson is recorded to have said: "I would wish to leave the ultimate origin of a tale... with a large question mark rather than a dubious answer".

Functionalism, proposed by Bronislaw Malinowski and Radcliffe Brown, is of the view that any cultural activity must have a utilitarian value for its people. Functionalists see the society as a stable entity perpetuated by the various cultural activities. Narratives are then seen as embodiment of the beliefs, customs, rituals and structures that need to be maintained. The narratives are also charged with the role of censuring deviants. William Bascom summarises this approach when he says:

> Folklore operates within a society to insure conformity to the accepted cultural norms and continuity from generation to generation through its role in education and the extent to which it mirrors culture. To the extent to which folklore contrasts with the accepted norms and offers socially accepted forms of release through amusement or humour and through creative imagination or fantasy, it tends to preserve the institutions from direct attack and change.

Functionalism is by far the most persistent theory in the study of oral literature. It in effect proposes an absolutist way of looking at life as a construct maintained by selected immutable principles and perhaps processes that must be perpetuated. But societies of course change and accommodate contemporary thought.

In fact neo-functionalists Raymond Firth and Edmund Leach state that society is not in functional unity but that there are always mitigating "emergent conflicts". From a sociological point of view, conflict is in fact necessary and inevitable for society to function. In which case, the fact that there is always conflict when there is apparent consensus means that the society is in a state of functional disunity, a view held by structural functionalists.

Then there is **formalism**, an approach propagated by Vladimir Prop and which is essentially a modification of diffusionism. It identifies the motifs in narratives and seeks to analyse the inter-character relationships in facilitating plots. Rather than looking at one tale, formalism is concerned with the form of groups of tales falling into one scheme.

An example of a formalist analysis is in Eleazor Maletinsky's essay, *"Marriage: Its Functions and Position in Folktales"*. She identifies that the first function in a tale with the motif of marriage is that a king's daughter is abducted, which is a violation of the traditional norms. This leads to the second function with a volunteer rescuing her from the abductors. The volunteer is rewarded by being given her as a wife. The conflict is resolved and the society's dignity restored.

This approach is essentially a sequential analysis of a narrative with highlights on the causative factors and the role of characters in the antecedents. In her study of Mende trickster narratives, Marion Kilson came up with a finding that the tale can be divided into: the initial phase which introduces the situation and the protagonists; the 'medial phase' involving the means of disposing off the problem; and the 'final phase' which is the resolution of the conflict. In the author's view, the formalistic stages in a narrative are not only three but five, namely: the initial stage when things are normal; the conflict stage when the problem arises to disrupt the prevailing order; the critical stage when characters sort themselves out into antagonistic camps; the climatic stage when the conflict cruises to a head; and the final stage when a resolution is reached. This structure is exemplified in the section on structure and style with the story "The Floating Gourd".

The last theory noted here is **structuralism**. Claude Levis Strauss, the foremost proponent of this theory, sees culture as a unit consisting of conjoined elements. In applying this to the study of myths, he says that myths are attempts by man to understand and resolve the contradictions in reality. To him all myths belong to a complex matrix of explanatory tales that must be analysed ethnologically if we are to appreciate the philosophies in them.

He proposes that ethnographic data should not be treated in isolation but should be compared across communities.

According to structuralists, characters in myths are embodiments of contradictory concepts such as life and death. Dominique Zahen simplified the structure of Life and Death tales and concluded that such stories rest on the basis that: the divine world is separate from the temporal and secular; there is emptiness between these two worlds and hence the need for a communicative link; there are malignant forces in the space and that these forces distract the agents of communication leading to a distortion of communication; and that the final resolution is that life and death have to co-exist just as other contradictions.

In many tales dealing with the struggle between life and death, we get an animal that is sent with the message that should ensure man's longevity. This animal gets messed up on the way and another agent delivers the opposite message. The disgraced animal is usually the chameleon. Referring to Henri Junod's work on South African culture, Zahen established that the chameleon is perceived as the "incarnation of two contradictory concepts of life and death re-united in one and the same being. Interestingly, this construct is observed in the reproduction process of a chameleon. The mother chameleon bursts and dies to give birth.

Our overview, rather than drawing a hard and fast line among the theories, is to illustrate their complementariness. They are like the six blind men of the orient who touched the elephant at different parts of the body. Each had his own idea of the configuration of the elephant, but each was only partly correct. The same with the theories. They should be seen to be complementary in understanding the nature of the narrative.

(Information used for this section was adapted from Isidore Okpewho's *Myth in Africa* and a polemical paper, *"Orature: Towards an Exegesis"*, presented to the staff and students of Egerton University, Laikipia College on February 20, 1991).

CLASSIFICATION OF NARRATIVES

In classification, let us first of all see how the existing Kenyan texts group narratives. Odaga and Akivaga come up with the following categories: Myths, Legends, Aetiological, Trickster, Monster and Dilemma narratives.[2] Nandwa and Bukenya on the other hand have: Myths, Legends, Fables, Ogre tales and Human tales.[3] Kipury has: Myths, Legends, Ogre, Trickster and other animal tales and finally Man stories.[4]

There is no difference, apart from that of terminology, between Kipury's and Nandwa and Bukenya's classification. That one of Odaga and Akivaga, however, differs: It separates 'myths' and 'aetiological narratives' and also includes 'Dilemma narratives'.

Before considering the various possible approaches to classification, it is proper to look at this question of 'myth'.

Ruth Finnegan says that 'Myth' is not a distinctive African genre and that it is a European imposition on African Orature. In European classification, she says, 'Myths' are:

> Narratives believed in some sense or other to be true, and concerned with the origin of things or the activities of deities.[5]

And she says that they differ from "folktales or ordinary stories (fictional narratives, taken much less seriously)"[6]. She also mentions that in African societies, sometimes there is no conscious or rigid classification and narratives are just lumped together. Thus she suggests that researchers should largely go by the people's own attitude towards their own oral literature in the task of classification as there seems to be no universal system.

As much as these observations are true and stimulating, the word 'myth' has persisted and continues to be used. It is therefore self-defeating to attempt truncating it from African Oral Literature lexis. Rather, it needs a delimitation for clarity of reference. After all, words are but arbitrary symbols that mean what people ascribe to them. Taking that then as a starting point, here are what other scholars think myths are.

According to Nandwa and Bukenya,

> Myths often attempt to explain the beginning of time, and are concerned with the projection of external principles as observed through natural phenomena... consist of events which happened in the distant sacred past, frequently related to the time of creation... the old testimonies... (including) Legendary, sometimes fictional lives of Heroes... (Interpreting) the relationships between the normal and the supernatural... (explaining) mysteries which lie beyond human understanding... They become records of society's beliefs. There are also aetiological myths which explain the origin of cultural traits and natural features[7].

Odaga and Akivaga see a myth as:

> a story that explains the origin of a group of people or tells something about the early development of a group of people. Certain myths explain the origin of... death, birth, creation of humanity, work, e.t.c. Most myths tell us about sacred beings and divine heroes. They are closely connected to the religious beliefs and practices of a people. They reveal the existence of spirits and supernatural powers... seen as having been instrumental in making things happen at the very beginning.[8]

Meanwhile, Kipury says that myths are "narratives that explain the origin of various phenomena"[9] and closely goes along with Odaga and Akivaga.

These definitions agree on certain characteristics of myths viz: they are based on the remote past and concern the origins; they try to explain the involvement of supernature in the early processes and the mysteries which baffle the human mind.

But then the scholars differ on the boundaries. Nandwa and Bukenya, basing themselves on the premise that myths include the fictional lives of heroes, include the story of Luanda Magere (Luo) under myths while the others group it under legends. Then they also consider the secular tales about natural phenomena under myths while Odaga and Akivaga label these as aetiological tales. The principal question then is: where does myth end and aetiology begin? Aren't all myths essentially aetiological? For example consider the narrative below:

Man Must Die

Nyasaye - Nyakalaga - Were - Akumu (God) wanted to put a stop to the rampages of death – death which claims the lives of everyone...

So one day he sent a servant to earth with a message for all his people; "Send me an offering of fresh untainted fat", he ordered. "It should be as clean and as sparkling as the moon". Hearing this, the people slaughtered a goat, removed its pure white fat, and placed it in a clay dish over-smeared with fine fresh leaves.

Now they summoned Ng'ongruok, also known as Haniafu the chameleon, and ordered him to take their offering to Nyasaye. They also fashioned a long pole that reached up to heaven where Nyasaye dwells in his glory. This was the path Ng'ongruok would follow when carrying their offerings.

But Ng'ongruok accidentally soiled the fat with his clumsy feet, and on his arrival before Nyasaye presented a dirty and unsightly offering. Nyasaye was furious and rejected it, shouting: "Tell the people of the earth that because of this insult, they must continue to die, just as their ancestors have done".

Ng'ongruok descended from heaven, delivered Nyasaye's message, and returned the offering to the people. Ever since then, alas, death has continued to ravage mankind. For his clumsiness, Ng'ongruok was cursed by people. Hence he always walks on all fours, and his steps must be hesitant and slow. That is why you will always see him carrying one leg raised from the ground as he tries to decide exactly where to tread.[10]

This, according to the Luo, explains why people continue to die – and should as such be classified as myth. But it has got at the end an aetiological twist, so to speak, and attempts to explain the posture of the chameleon. Why should it not be classified as aetiological? The problem with such a narrative may be less if the intention of the narrator is known as

140

may be gleaned from the title he gives the story. "Man Must Die" as a title lays stress on death and so places the narrative as 'myth' by Odaga and Akivaga's classification. But if it were 'Why the chameleon walks hesitantly', then it would qualify as aetiological. Left blank, the onus is on the researcher to put the label.

In this text, the author takes the standpoint that myth includes all accounts of the origin of time, creation, deities and the occurrence of natural and cultural traits in the environment. This encompasses both the sacred and the secular etiological accounts.

Reverting to the larger question of classification, Odaga and Akivaga, Kipury and Finnegan advise that it is difficult to come up with a conclusive scheme. But even if that is generally true, it is important that a classification be consistent in the criterion or criteria used such that we do not have in the same space a narrative classified using characters, another using content and another by the effect it is intended to produce in the audience.

Below then is a discussion of some approach to classification.

Plot Classification

This is an engagement associated with the diffusionists who try to trace the narrative plots to their historical and geographical origins. They recognise for example the 'tug-of-war' motif to be African. But even without giving this kind of continental genealogy, several motifs can be identified e.g.

The Jealous Step-mother

A jealous step-mother tries to get rid of her step-child whose mother has died. However, the victim survives out of some salvaging act of the favoured child or some peers. The jealous woman gets punished by the husband.

The Jealous Peers

A group of girls go to a beautician. One girl's beauty is outstanding and she instantly attracts the males. The peers are disheartened and they mistreat her by changing her into various articles and even burying her, in some cases. However, she survives and lives on.

The Tug of War

A small animal, usually Hare, invites two huge animals to a contest. Each of the latter thinks it is pulling the hare not knowing it is actually pulling its peer. At the end of the game, Hare goes to each for acknowledgement of his 'strength'.

The Sacrificial Girl

A community faces drought and famine. The oracle ordains that a human sacrifice be made. The village beauty is named as the sacrifice. The family finds this a grievous demand and yet they have to succumb. In some tales the girl gets consumed while in others she is salvaged by her lover and they go and live elsewhere.

The Journey to Heaven

Two friendly animals, usually Hare and Spider, go as suitors to heaven. Spider is the groom and Hare an accompanying friend. Hare tries some trick and a disagreement results in Spider folding its web and leaving Hare stranded there. The latter jumps to earth and gets injured but lives on.

The Fallen Hero

A legendary warrior gets undone after careful schemes by the enemies.

The Shepherd and His Special Animal

A shepherd is abducted and taken to a foreign country. Attempts made to poison him are revealed to him by a pet calf he has and he eventually escapes back to his homeland.

Many more motifs can be identified but the above suffice to illustrate the point. Let us now look at the following three narratives from three communities to appreciate the point. They fall under the jealous step-mother motif.

Step Mother (Luo)

A man had two daughters from two different wives. One of his daughters was motherless, her mother died when she was still a baby. The mother of the other daughter did not like the motherless girl. She did not like her because her father loved her very much and also because her daughter loved her step-sister more than she loved her. Above all she was jealous of the motherless girl because she was very pretty. The woman therefore thought out some ways of eliminating her.

One day the woman made an arrangement with a hyena. The hyena was to go and wait for the two girls, somewhere in the bush. To the motherless girl she would tie a band like a bungle on the left arm and to her own daughter she would tie one on the right. Then she told hyena to catch, kill and eat the girl with the band on the left arm. After the hyena had gone to wait, she called the two girls, tied the bands accordingly and sent both of them to go and visit one of their aunts. She directed them to follow the path where she had asked the hyena to wait for them.

On the way the woman's daughters suggested that they should exchange bungles.

"Why should my mother tie your bungle on the left arm, when everybody else wears theirs on the right arm?" She complained and took her bungle and put it on her step-sister's right arm and took the one she was wearing and put it on her left arm. They went on with their journey.

They had gone half-way through the journey when the hyena came and caught the woman's own daughter and ate her up. The motherless child was terrified and grew hysterical. She cried endlessly. Her grief was so great that she refused to go away from the scene of her sister's tragic death. She wished to die too; to be eaten up by the hyena which had eaten her dear friend and sister. She cried, wailed, wept and grieved for her dear sister, so much that if sorrow expressed by the living would bring back the dead, Awino's sister Nyawino, would have returned to life. After the kill the hyena had gone away but Awino would not leave. She stayed on the spot wailing.

"Aai, what are you doing here alone in the bush?" some travellers asked her.

"We were two, and we were going to visit our aunt, but my sister has been eaten up by a hyena," she replied amid sobs.

"Then what are you doing here alone? Go home and take the sad news of her death to your parents," the people advised her.

"No, I also want to be eaten up by the same hyena," she cried. The travellers saw her futile determination. They could not leave her there and in any case, they were convinced that the parents should know.

"No, you go home and take the news of the death of your sister home," the people advised her more persuasively until she accepted to go home.

She arrived home, tired and wet with tears and sweat. She explained what had happened to her father. He became furious and called his wife to explain. But she was so full of grief that she could not talk. The elders were then called. It was agreed unanimously that the woman must be banished from the village because of her jealousy and wickedness. She left the village crying with regret and shame.[11]

Two Step-brothers Who Were Friends (Maasai)

There once lived two step-brothers who were such close friends that no one could separate them. One of the boys lost his mother at an early age, so the surviving

143

woman was charged with the responsibility of taking care of both the boys. And the woman who was the boy's step-mother had no liking for her step-son. And the boy's duty was to look after cattle, among which was one gentle cow that the boys used to milk each day whenever they became hungry. Each of the boys drew from the cow's two teats, and this became a rule which they always observed. The boys referred to each other as "son of my father" because they were the sons of one man.

Their mother, as the surviving woman came to be called by both boys, did not like the idea of the two boys being such good friends and so tried unsuccessfully to separate them. She said to herself, "I must find a way of killing this boy". So the next day as the boys took the cattle out grazing, she told her son to return home in the middle of the day to have a hair cut. The boy did as he was bid, and at around midday he went back home, had a hair cut, drank some milk and returned to the cattle. The next day it was the turn of the other boy to have his hair cut. But before they went home, the woman dug a deep hole at the head of the bed. On arrival the boy was sent to fetch a razor at the head of the bed. But as he tried to rummage through for the blade, he fell into the hole which the woman quickly covered with a big stone. The other boy waited expectantly for his friend until evening when he drove the cattle back home, assuming that his friend may have been assigned some other duty at home.

As soon as he got home, he looked for his step-brother, but on not finding him, he asked his mother where he was. She categorically denied having any knowledge of his whereabouts, saying, "I gave him a hair cut and he went back to the cattle". The people looked for the boy everywhere, and when they could not find him, they assumed he had been eaten by wild animals.

After some time the villagers went home and burnt up the old village. When the rains fell, some long grass grew at the old settlement. One day, the surviving boy, who had cried until he could cry no more for his brother, took the cattle there to graze. While the cattle grazed, he went and sat down at the big stone that covered the hole inside which was his brother. And so it happened that the boys had a song they used to sing when they were milking their cow. As he sat on the stone, they boy remembered his step brother and he started the song:

> Son of my father
> The udder of the dapple grey is bursting with milk
> But I will not draw your teats
> Son of my father.

When the boy in the hole heard the other one singing, he responded to him in song:

> Son of my father
> You may draw and let it nurture you
> Son of my father
> You may draw and let it nurture you
> For it was your mother who put me into the hole

When the boy on top of the stone first heard the reply, he thought his voice was simply being echoed by the forest. He sang one more time, and again his brother sang in response, and he realised that the singing was coming from underneath the stone. On rolling the stone away, he was astonished to see his brother whom he helped out of the hole. He had eaten soil and his clothes were all tattered. He could barely see, for his eyes had grown sensitive to the light. The boy gave his brother one of his sheets to put on, and he milked one of the cows for him to drink fresh milk. He first made him vomit all the soil he had been eating, and then fed him with some fresh milk. When evening came he took him home with him.

On their way home, the boy who had been rescued related to his step-brother how their mother had put him inside the hole. His step-brother became furious because he loved his brother more than any other person. When they were about to reach home, he sharpened his spear till it was razor sharp. On arrival, he headed straight for his mother, whom he instantly speared to death. He next sought his father to inform him of what he had done. The men were then assembled, and when the story was told, the people simply listened without comment. Nothing could be done. So the boys lived happily without a mother.[12]

Nyaga and Wamweru (Gikuyu) *by Muthee Mugo*

A man had two wives. The first gave birth to a boy she called Nyaga and a girl called Wamweru. The other gave birth to a girl called Wacici. The first wife died. Nyaga used to look after his father's animals. The two girls used to stay at home. The father decided that he would decorate the girl who had lost the mother. The girl was given necklaces and beads. The living woman was angry because the same was not done to her daughter.

Now the mother discussed with the daughter and decided to bury the other girl so that the girl could do what with the stool? Sit on it. Now Wacici and the mother dug a hole in the store, it was Wacici and the mother who did this.

145

Wamweru was sent and she never imagined that a hole had been dug. Wacici took the stool. She sat on it. Now the girl came and asked for her stool and it was refused with. She was asked by the step-mother, "Why are you asking for the stool? Sit on that oiled skin. It is better than this stool". Now the girl went and did what? She sat on the skin. She sank. They covered the hole. She was buried with the skin. She was buried.

Haya, the other girl stayed there with the mother. They cooked. They cooked. The young man Nyaga came. He sat down. When he sat down, he asked, "Where is Wamweru? He was told, "I sent Wamweru". They ate the food. They ate the food. Wamweru had not come. The next day the boy asked her, "Where did Wamweru go?" And because he used to sit on the garden at night to check the animals, he was told, "Wamweru did not sleep here. I don't know where she is, maybe she got married. "Ai, she has stayed!" He sat down. He was told the father was not at home. When the father came and asked where the girl was, he was told that she had been sent and didn't come back. The woman said that maybe the girl got married. Now the father stayed and knew that the girl was lost completely. He said, "I shall move from this home where my child got lost. I wouldn't want anything like this to happen". They left the place. When they moved, a big bush grew where the home was. Now the boy used to go there to graze the goats. As they wanted to enter the bush, he told them,

> You Gicheru don't go into that Iganjo.
> (bushes that grow on an old homestead)

The girl who was underground heard and said:

> You child who abuses the goat?
> We used to drink blood together?
> We used to drink, I was buried by your mother
> because of beads
> divider of milk

The girl sang from underground. The boy was silent; he was silent. He shouted at the goat again.

> Hi Gicheru don't go to that Iganjo.

The girl sang again.

The boy kept quiet and brought home the livestock and told the father, "Father, our girl who got lost has been singing. Let us go tomorrow and you listen". That is how the father went with the child. He went and they shouted at the goats.

146

You Gicheru don't go into that bush where people got lost.

The girl sang:

> Hi Gicheru don't go to that Iganjo.

The girl sang again:

> Hi Gicheru don't go to that Iganjo.

The girl sang again.

Haya, the man got a stick and made a ladder and went down the hole, he went and the girl came up. "I have nothing. I am naked." He came and brought her clothes. Now the girl did what? She came out. She was taken out and brought to the garden. The boy took the livestock home, the man prepared his daughter. She vomited, she vomited soil and all the beads she ate when she was underground. The decorations she had been wearing.

Now the man went home. Ugali was prepared for the man by the woman. He told the woman and the daughter to eat that ugali. The mother became a hyena and the girl a fox.

It is important to note there could be variants of the same story within the same community.

Classification by motif is a very interesting but also tiring and tedious activity. Where one does not have an extensive corpus, it becomes inconclusive as he can't group the narratives and identify the motifs. All the same it is a useful approach especially in comparative studies.

Content Classification

This is the system of grouping the narratives according to their subjects. It is the approach from which we get such classes:

a) Myth – tales tinted with religion, superstition and traditional beliefs especially about the origins of mankind and other phenomena.

b) Legends – stories about historical events and memorable people e.g. war heroes, outstanding medicinemen, migration, e.t.c.

c) Fiction – imaginary tales. This category may be divided into allegory, fables, fantasy, parables e.t.c. The label 'fiction' should not exclude the first two; myth and legend. Rather, these two are told as if they were true and unchallengeable. Whereas the credibility of myths is less distinct, that of legends is much more corroborable, the events having happened in the not very distant past. What we have labelled 'fiction' here are the purely imaginary tales.

Classification by Social Function or Institution

This stems from the functional theories that see narratives as vehicles of cultural instructions. The stories are then grouped according to their institutions such as:

Political Stories

Stories about leadership and the relationship between leaders and their subjects. A good example is the following story of Odera Akang'o from the Luo.

> Odera Akang'o was a chief in Gem of Siaya District. He was a very industrious and autocratic ruler. He ensured that everyone worked on his shamba and produced food. Among the many things he achieved were: planting of trees along roads, introduction of western-type education and propagation of christianity. Most of these innovations arose from his travels to Uganda. He is reputed to have been very impatient with people who liked eating a lot of food. He would give such a fellow so much food which failure to finish led to severe caning.
>
> To some people he was unpopular due to his dictatorship. It is also said that he was very fond of taking people's wives and their property by force. Thus he was accused to the colonial government, indicted and detained at Kismayu. He was later transferred to Nairobi where he died in the year 1918.[14]

Clan System

Stories here reveal the structures of families and communities i.e. genealogies, marriage, e.t.c. Here is an example from the Maasai.

> In the beginning there was Naiteru-Kop, the beginner of the earth. He married two wives giving the first one red cattle and the name Nado-Mong'i. Her house was built on the right-hand side of the gateway. The second Narok-Kiteng' was given black cattle and her house was built on the left-hand side of the gateway.
>
> After some time they both gave birth. The first wife had three sons and named the first Lelian, the second Lokesen and the third Losero. From these sons arose the Ilmolelian, Ilmakesen and Iltaarrosero clans. These are called the clans of the right hand following the location of their mother's house.
>
> The second wife had two sons, Leiser and Lukum. These are the progenitors of the Aiser and Lukumai clans. They form the left hand clans.
>
> Each clan developed its own system of branding cattle to distinguish them from the others. These systems are still being followed.[15]

Religion and Deities

Tales about creation and phenomena like rain, death, e.t.c. fall here. Here is an example again from the Maasai:

> There were two gods: the black god and the red god. The former was humble and loving while the latter was malevolent. The black god lived below the red god in the heaven and so nearer to men.
>
> Once when there was a drought, and famine, the black god conferred with the red god if they could give water to human beings. After much pleading they agreed to do so and it rained.
>
> After sometime the red god suggested that they withdraw the rain since man had had enough. The black god however asked for an extension until the second time when the red god repeated the request and they stopped the rain.
>
> When some days had passed, the black god again asked for rain but the red god refused. They started arguing with the red god threatening vengeance on man and the black god restraining him. So when we hear the sound of loud thunder, it is the red god struggling to get past the black god. And when the thunder is not so loud, it is the black god trying to prevent the wrath of the red god.[16]

Moral Virtues

Some stories are meant to deride such vices as greed, pride, thievery, foolishness, lack of insight, murder, dishonesty, e.t.c Below is an example from the Gikuyu.

> There was a man with two sons – Kiongo and Meciria. He wanted to test their wisdom. So he called and gave each of them an egg. They wanted to take the eggs to be cooked by their mother. But the father talked to them saying: "Take your eggs and find a secret place where no one can see you... go there and break the egg."
>
> They rose up the next morning and went to the forest. Kiongo broke his egg where no one could see him. Meciria on the other hand found a place but before he broke the egg, he thought that the father actually wanted to test if they could do bad things as long as they were not seen.
>
> He rushed home and told his father who was very happy of the boy's insight.[17]

Economics

We have stories that deal with work, borrowing and lending, industriousness and laziness e.t.c. A good instance is the Luo story below.

A certain hare once lived with his grandmother. The time for sowing came and the old lady sent the hare to the farm. But he was lazy and did not like the work. He cheated the granny by saying that peas grow best when first roasted before being planted. The grandmother did as she was advised.

Every morning the hare would go to the garden, eat all the peas and put dust on his feet and then go home feigning tiredness. When the granny went to check on the farm, she saw only weeds but the hare assured her that she had gone to the wrong plot.

When time for harvesting came, Hare decided to steal from his uncle's farm. Arriving home with the loot, the grandmother was convinced that he had been saying the truth. But one time the uncle put a trap and Hare fell victim. But then he used trickery to save himself.

There was an eagle flying overhead at that time. Hare pretended that he was on a swing. Eagle got attracted to this and begged to be allowed to join in. He released Hare and got into the 'swing'. As soon as he was firmly tied, Hare started shouting and calling his uncle that he had caught the thief.

The uncle arrived and dealt Eagle death blows. He took it home for a meal and rewarded Hare with a lot of crop.

This tale talks about the institution of work and basically castigates indolence.

So many of these institutions can be identified. The main hitch is that of overlapping. The question of moral virtues permeate a majority of the narratives and it is neither easy nor logical to label some as moralising and others not. Like the foregoing narrative also criticises theft and lack of insight which leads Eagle into trouble.

Characterological Classification

This approach categorises the stories according to the dominant characters in them. Titles like 'Trickster Narratives' are derived from this approach. To be more comprehensive we can identify the following classes:

i) Human Tales: stories in which human beings are the main characters.

ii) Animal Tales: those in which the animals are the more important characters. The stories are also called 'fables'.

iii) Ogre or Monster Tales: where a hideous, gigantic and grotesque creature plays the leading role.

iv) Spirit Tales: in which invisible and supernatural powers influence the course of events.

v) Stories about deities: those which acknowledge the involvement of community gods in the events.

vi) Stories about inanimate objects: in which non-animal characters play leading roles e.g. trees, stones, e.t.c.

Of course one comes across the tales that include a cross section of all these characters. Then he has to evaluate their significance before deciding on his classification.

Traditional Classification

This approach is research and contact based. The classification is done the way the mother community does it. Finnegan suggests "modest research" into African Literature for the documentation of the typologies of society's Orature. She gives examples of traditional classes from the Kimbundu of Angola, viz:

1) *Misoso* – "stories regarded as fictitious... arising from imagination" and meant principally to entertain and exercise the mind. "The class includes animal tales and stories about the marvelous and supernatural".

2) *Maka* – "reputedly true stories or anecdotes.. instructive... entertaining and are socially didactic, concerned with how to live and act".

3) *Malunda or Misendu* – "the chronicles of the tribe and nation transmitted by headmen or elders... historical narratives.[18]

Kabira and Mutahi go along with the approach and identify the following classes among the Gikuyu:

1) *Ng'ano* – (narratives) but used to mean "history, biographies, autobiographies, heroic narratives and stories of origin.

2) *Ng'ano cia marimū* – "(ogre narratives), used to mean all fictional narratives i.e. they are creations of the mind and the narrator has no illusion about their factuality. There may even be no ogre in the story but it still falls under the category.[19]

This particular approach goes down to the root of the material as cultural products. But a scholar needs to transcend the acknowledgement and delve into other schemes when dealing with material from more than one community.

As it were, a comprehensive approach can also be adopted with narratives such that the scholar/researcher uses all the discussed criteria in his job as exemplified with poetry.

151

STRUCTURE AND STYLE

Performance

In talking about performance, we look at who tells the stories, when, where and how. Each community has its own system but certain similarities exist among them and recur with noticeable regularity. In his anthology, *Myths and Legends of the Congo*, Jan Knappert describes the narrative situation in Africa thus:

> There are many ways of telling stories in Africa. Usually it's after nightfall that the call can be heard, "Tell a story storyteller!" There must be a fire to sit round and the storyteller is mostly an elderly person who "has forgotten more than you have seen in your life". There are special expressions in use for begging a storyteller to begin his story, and once he has started, to make him go on. In the middle of the story the narrator will stop and refuse to go on unless more tobacco is provided, for without a smoking pipe, the ideas will not come.[20]

This idyllic description gives a bird's eye view of what happens before and during narration. For purposes of our analysis, we shall divide the narrative occasion into three phases namely:

i) Pre-narration phase
ii) Narration phase
iii) Post-narration phase

Pre-narration Phase

Before any narration occurs, there are preconditions that are established. There must first of all be the need for storytelling, a purpose to be served e.g. entertainment or social instruction. This may not be explicitly stated but is implied and indeed demanded by the social context in that certain situations create an ideal atmosphere for storytelling.

Secondly, there must be a person with a story to tell – a narrator, and whom to tell it to – an audience. One doesn't tell a story to oneself. Following this precondition, there must be a convergence of these parties at a place or through some medium that accords opportunity for the telling and listening.

The place of narration differs from community to community. Knappert recognises that the Congo do it sitting round a fire. In Kenya, the Maasai sit in an open ground generally used for other purposes. The Luo on the other hand, principally tell stories in the 'siwindhe' – grandmother's hut, where the maidens sleep. But it can also be in the 'duol' – the special hut for the male head of the homestead. Here the narratives told mainly dwell on History, Religion, and legendary people. Whatever the place is, the significant point is that the participants gather somewhere which has to be agreeable to all and convenient if not also comfortable – a relaxed atmosphere.

A third precondition is the availability of time. The time available must be free of other distractions and in essence determine the kind of story told in terms of length and the number of stories told at that one sitting.

Finally, for the occasion to succeed, it must be bound by certain conventions to guide the participants. These conventions stretch from beliefs to practical procedures. One common custom is that stories should not be told during the day. This ethic is found for example among the Luo, Maasai and Gikuyu. The Luo believe that telling stories at day time leads to retarded growth of the teller and the Maasai that it leads to loss of cattle as the Gikuyu that all cattle, sheep and goats would mysteriously disappear and a particular tribe, clan or family become irredeemably poor.[21]

The basic idea behind these beliefs is that daytime should be used for other chores against which storytelling would be a distraction. However, they give us a glimpse about the social perspectives of the groups. The Luo's fear of being retarded expresses their admiration for height. And indeed the Luo are generally tall people, not for adhering to the ethic necessarily. From the Maasai and Gikuyu, it is clear that livestock are considered as wealth and regarded very highly.

To usher in the narration phase, certain overtures take place. People would for example chit-chat or trade riddles before coming to serious narration. These are techniques of adjusting the mind to the mood of the time and preparing the person for the expected. Among the Luo there is a marked beginning of the narration phase by a call to order by the eldest person in the group announcing:

> Ot mondo odhi kwath
> Ot mondo odhi tun'g
> Ot mondo oduog diere
> Ot mondo olin'g thi

> Let the house go grazing
> Let the house go to the end
> Let the house come to the centre
> Let the house be dead silent.

This is a pattern the author has only encountered among the Luo. Other groups may or may not have it and probably have alternatives. This structure may be called the **salutatory formula**.

Then there occurs the fixed expression announced to the commencement of a narrative. It is in most cases an exchange between the narrator and his audience. Finnegan records that a Limba narrator calls out to his audience by name and the named person repeats the name before the narrator starts the story. She records:

Suri – reply to me. I am going to tell a story... (names the story). I am going to tell it this evening. You Yenkeni, by your grace, you are to reply to me.[22]

Suri and Yenkeni are members of the audience.

The Luo narrator will instead ask *"Agannue?"* – "May I tell you a story" and the audience replies, *"Gannua"* – "Tell us a story". Such expressions are called **opening formulas**. Ruth Finnegan records in her epic book the following examples:

1. *Fjort: West Equatorial Africa*
   Narrator: Let's be off
   Audience: Pull away.

2. *Ewe: Ghana*
   (The narrator beats a small drum for a short while and then says: My story is so-and-so)

3. *Akan: Ghana*
   Narrator: We do not really mean, we do not really mean (that what we are going to say is true).

4. *Hausa: Nigeria*
   Narrator: A story, a story, let it go, let it come, or, see her (the spider), see her there.
   Audience: Let her come and let us hear.

5. *Nilyamba: Central Africa*
   Narrator: A story. How does it go?[23]

An opening formula has its aesthetic and stylistic functions. First of all, it is a verbal contract between the narrator and the audience – the former seeks the permission of the latter. The latter's assent launches the two into a business of narrating and listening. The formula also directs the attention of the audience to the narrator i.e. where the narration is rotational, it identifies the next narrator. The narrator defines what he is going to do – tell a story, and hence binds himself to the contract to do nothing else but that, until his time is over.

The other important guideline is the rotation in the storytelling. It is understood by all that the narration is not one person's monopoly but an interaction. One person stops and another starts off in an orderly sequence as per the sitting or sleeping arrangement. It may not be compulsory that one tells a story at his turn although it is only prestigious to do so and embarrassing otherwise. Among the Luo, one who is not able to narrate just then excuses himself saying: *"Hasigro jaleny thee"* meaning, "The potsherd fizzles *thee*"; the narrative has evaporated from his mind the same way that butter melts on the hot potsherd.

Narration Phase

In the narration of a story there is a triangular interaction of the narrative, narrator and the audience. The narrative is the raw material. It has to be processed and put across to someone. The narrator is the medium of conveyance and the audience is the recipient. The relationship may be presented diagrammatically as follows:

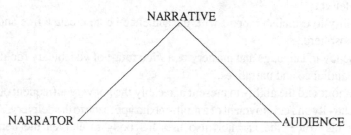

A successful story should be interesting. This depends on whether it is short or long, familiar or unfamiliar, fixed or elastic and fictional or factual. The appreciation of a story highly depends on the age of the audience. The youngsters tend to enjoy more the adventurous stories e.g. the exploits of tricksters.

Familiarity of a narrative determines the attention the audience gives it. An audience generally prefers a new narrative. But then the familiarity also plays a positive role as it makes the audience authoritative in their mastery of the episodes. Therefore they are able to guide a narrator who is missing out or misrepresenting a narrative. It also enables them participate more effectively, for example in the singing of the song parts. Again, it must be noticed that however familiar a narrative is, it is a fresh creation every other time it is told. Even the same narrator telling the same story at different times actually does it differently. Thus a familiar story is not always a bore. In fact, some of them are so breathtaking, the audience keeps demanding their repetition.

The length of the narrative comes in when considering the attention span of the audience. Children may not easily follow long-winded and intricate stories. The narrator abridges such narratives to suit them. When a narrative may also be too short, he can work round and lengthen it by repetition and such-like devices.

The narrator as such plays a central role in the success of a narrative. Therefore his abilities have to be put into focus. People are endowed with diverse abilities which predetermine their potentialities beyond which they can never excel. But each one puts his talents to the best effect. With or without the talents and limitations, an audience does not need prompting to recognise a good narrator. Such a narrator may be marked out by the following qualities:

1. Familiarity with and ability to refer to his culture and environment to enliven the narrative and make it appeal to the audience.
2. A good memory for accurate retention and narration of a large corpus of material.
3. Knowledge of the audience and its needs. This includes the age, level of motivation and preferences to determine the choice of the narrative and technique of delivery.
4. Ability to establish rapport with the audience i.e. to create a free and informal atmosphere.
5. Fluency in language and mastery of a wide range of vocabulary for all levels of the audience and narratives.
6. Candour and the ability to present agreeably the not very infrequent obscenities.
7. Creativity and employment of a multi-media approach to the delivery. Apart from just his voice, the narrator also uses his body to enliven the performance. Narration is not only speech but actually drama. The narrator creates the characters and presents them to the audience through mimicry. Jan Knappert puts it this way:

> All the characters of the drama are introduced with their own voices: the wild pig's snorting, the snake's hissing, the bird's fluting, the lion's lazy yawn.[24]

This means that the narrator must be a very versatile person in his tone of voice, speed of delivery, e.t.c. and just nothing but dynamic.

The third factor, the audience, is integral in the narration. A narrative audience is usually active. It catalyses the narrative by spontaneous exclamations, questions to the narrator, echoing of the narrator's voice, joining in the singing of choruses, e.t.c. For all these to take place, there must be discipline. The audience should be able to laugh, exclaim, but without jeopardising the continuation of the narration.

Having said all these, let us then have a feel of the interaction of the narrator, narrative and audience by quoting and illustrating some records from Kabira and Mutahi's story, "The New Mother". In this tale, a new mother is taunted by an ogre in the absence of her husband who has gone to smith in the forest.

> Now they set off together and went and built a blacksmith's booth, where? Far away from home.

When the narrator asks "where?", he is inviting the audience's response by which means he detects and monitors their attention.

In the husband's absence, the ogre comes.

> The ogre would then cook and cook some food. It would cook and eat. Would the new mother be well fed with the little bit she is given? She would be given very little while the rest would be grabbed by the ogre while still saying, "Do take some new mother's feed".

Here we get the same rhetoric and the quotation of the ogre's words. Later on the mother is visited by some birds which she asks to deliver a message saying:

> Little birds
> If I give you millet to eat
> then send you
> would you go?
> Yes.
> Do you hear? They said Yes.

Here the narrator intervenes to ask the audience whether they hear the birds' reply in a manner as to build expectation in them for a turn of events by the coming of the birds.

> The birds did not refuse. They went and on arrival they said: cu cu cu cu cu cu, when on trees.

Notice the ideophonic recreation of what Knappert calls the "fluting of the birds". Having been convinced of the bird's message, the old man goes home.

> The old man did not spend any other night. He took his sword and spear. He took off, kurugucu kurugucu kurugucu. He went and arrived during the daylight. During the daylight like it is now.[25]

The ideophone "kurugucu" represents the hasty way the man moved. Then we notice the narrator's reference to daylight "like it is now" which tells us that the narrative was collected during the day and confirms that the narrator uses his environment for reference.

This is but a brief representation of the liveliness of a narration session. Another central issue concerning the narrator is that of age, sex and professionality. Generally, both adults and children tell stories but the latter are better accomplished and some particularly stand out above others. By oral transfer the children learn the stories, perpetuate them and also become adept in their own right. Sex-wise, again anybody would tell stories but there is a marked domination of the art by females in most Kenyan communities. The men would mainly specialise on historical and religious tales. But in some communities, there are expert male narrators as Finnegan notes in the Limba society and Kabira also does in her book, *The Oral Artist*.

The question of professionality may be looked at in two ways – that of artistic expertise and that of economic gain. A skilled and artistic story teller is a professional in the mastery of the art. But most times people talk of professionalism to mean the derivation of economic benefits from ones art. Finnegan says that:

> This has been asserted of, among others, the Temne, Hausa and Yoruba of West Africa, Yao of East Africa, and the Bulu, Rwanda and possibly the Pygmies of Central and West Equatorial Africa.[26]

She is however doubtful of the extent to which the storyteller earns his living from the art.

> In most instances there is no evidence that any material reward accrues to the story-teller, however great his expertise. Though some individuals are clearly regarded as more expert than others, storytelling tends to be a popular rather than a specialist art. All, it appears, are potentially expert storytellers, and are, with some limitations, prepared to take in the evening occasion when stories are being told and exchanged in social gatherings. There is no African parallel to the specialist privileged class of narrators to be found, say, in Polynesia.[27]

At least in Kenya, there are no records of professional narrators in the material economic sense. Story telling is largely a communal rather than separatist affair.

Post-narration Phase

At the end of a narrative the audience reacts in different ways. If it is a jocular romantic story, the reaction is likely to be laughter. On the other hand, a tragic story evokes feelings of melancholy leading to catharsis – an emotional purgation. The audience which has been held in suspense is brought down sighing with the finale.

When the narrator has enthused the audience, he may be asked for another story of a similar nature or to retell one told during an earlier occasion. This is very characteristic of children audiences. Otherwise he may simply be told to tell any story of his own choice.

As with the opening formula, there is also the **closing formula** that indicates the end of a story. Some examples are:

1. Gikuyu: Kenya
   (My story) ends there.

2. Luo: Kenya
   The end. May I grow as tall as the tree at my uncle's.

3. Kimbundu: Angola

   I have told my story, whether good or bad.[28]

4. Bura: Nigeria

   Don't take my life, take the life of a crocodile.[29]

These formulae are some kind of swear. In some of them are expressions of cultural standards. As we saw with the Luo admiration of height in the admonition against telling stories during the day, the final formula reiterates the desire for height. The narrator wishes to grow as tall as the tree at the uncle's (the maternal uncle). Why? A maternal uncle is held in very high regard in the Luo culture. He is supposed to be very intimate with his nephews and nieces. It is believed that if he canes them they become deaf. The closing formula expresses the desire for longevity, height and a preservation of that intimacy as an acknowledgement of that maternal genealogy.

After the formula ending one narrative, another person goes on with another narrative until such a time as the whole session comes to an end. The people disperse with a tacit agreement and projection to the next session. But again with the Luo, there is a special formula that brings to a close the evening's activities, recited by the eldest person thus:

> *Sigana go tielo*
> *Sigana go dhoot*
> *Sigana go tielo*
> *Sigana go widhi.*

> Tale end at bedroom
> Tale end at door
> Tale end at bedroom
> Tale end at ledge.

Corresponding to the salutatory formula, this may be called the **valedictory formula**. The three phases of narrative performance are summarised in the diagram below:

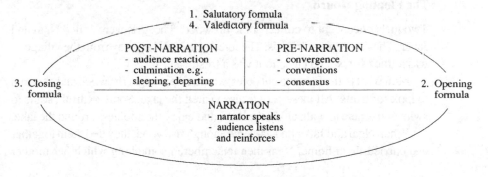

159

Narrative Layout

The narrative session falls into 5 segments namely:
1. Salutation
2. Opening formula
3. Narration
4. Closing formula
5. Valedictory formula

with allowance for variation among communities.

Coming to the narrative itself, there is a geographical structure of chronology of parts and events. This structure is what is called "plot" and it can be generally divided into five segments:

1. Initial situation: the existence of normal relationships e.g. friendship.
2. Conflict: a problem arises that disturbs the tranquility e.g. a disagreement between the friends.
3. Crisis: the problem mounts e.g. the former friends become morbid enemies and scheme against one another.
4. Climax: the complications have accumulated and reached their peak e.g. the foes converge for a showdown.
5. Denouement: the after-effects of the contest and resolution of the conflict e.g. one character defeats the other and reigns supreme or forces are at par and a reconciliation occurs.

This kind of structure may be called a linear plot – one thing leads to another logically to the end. The several episodes in the stream are joined by conjunctives like "after that"... "then"... e.t.c. This linearity makes it very easy to comprehend the tales and memorise them, especially since they are delivered orally and the oral medium is temporal.

Below is a narrative that excellently illustrates the linear plot.

The Floating Gourd

Two girls once went to collect some firewood. The girls were called Ngai and Jaber. They were great friends. The forest was very far away from the village. It was a thick forest and close to it was a freshwater lake.

Men went to the forest to cut poles, women went to get firewood and children to look for fruits. All these people also visited the lake. Some to drink, some to swim and others to walk along the shore and enjoy the coolness around the lake.

When Ngai and Jaber had gathered enough firewood, they tied them together and carried them home. Ngai then remembered something which her mother

160

once told her; "The lake sometimes brings good luck to girls who fetch firewood for their mothers. Therefore you must always turn and look at the lake whenever you carry firewood from the forest". **(Para. 1-3: Initial situation.)**

So Ngai who was walking behind Jaber, turned and looked at the lake. She saw a red gourd floating towards the shore. From the neck of the gourd hang many beads. She did not tell Jaber about the gourd. But she started to sing a song, asking the gourd to come to her. Jaber heard the song and she also began to sing it:

Come to me
You are my beautiful gourd.

The gourd immediately floated back into the lake. This happened several times. When Ngai sang, the gourd floated towards the shore, but when Jaber sang the gourd went back. A quarrel then broke out. Ngai and Jaber both wanted the gourd. **(Conflict)**

"The gourd does not want you, Jaber, don't you see that when you sing it runs away and when I sing it comes nearer", Ngai told Jaber.

"If I won't have it, why should I let you?" Jaber replied maliciously. While they quarrelled the gourd did not move forward or backward. Then came an old man. He did not see the gourd. **(Crisis.)**

"What are you girls quarrelling about?" he asked the girls.

"It is about the gourd which is on the water", Ngai answered as she pointed out to the gourd.

"What about it?" the old man asked again when he had located where the cause of the quarrel was.

"It is mine and if I sing to it, it will come. But this girl won't let me have it. When she sings, the gourd runs away", Ngai explained.

"I want both of you to sing and let me see for myself what happens", the old man said.

The girls stared at each other briefly and Ngai who was sure she was on the right sang first and the gourd moved nearer. Jaber hesitated, she knew what to expect and indeed when she sang, the gourd moved backwards.

"Ah! Now I see. But there is no need to quarrel. Let the gourd come to Ngai. It may contain something both of you can share and there is nothing better than sharing things. You must also know that we cannot all have the same things in life", the old man explained to Jaber. He was gentle and patient and he finally managed to change Jaber's mind. **(Climax.)**

161

She now saw things differently.

"I agree, Ngai can have the gourd", Jaber said humbly.

Ngai sang and Jaber kept quiet until the gourd arrived. Ngai tried to lift it out of the water but it was too heavy. She called Jaber to help her. It was a magic gourd and when it was put on the ground, it opened to produce cows, sheep and several other things. They were happy. They thanked the old man, who then helped them to drive the herds home, to the amazed villagers. After relating their story, the parents of Ngai and Jaber agreed to give the old man some cattle as gifts. He then helped them to divide the rest between themselves. That is how the two families became rich.[31] **(Denouement.)**

The linearity of the narrative is however not to demean the complexity of narrative plots.

Now let us consider the plot of the next narrative.

Hare and Antelope

There once lived a hare, who one day as she was sauntering about in the bush, found an arrow which she picked up. On her way back home, she came upon a group of hunters who were skinning an animal they had killed, and she said to them: "If you give me a fat piece of meat I will give you something nice in exchange". The hunters asked: "And what could that be?" Hare replied: "It is an arrow head given to me by God". Hare was given a fat piece of meat in exchange for the arrow head. She bid the hunters goodbye and went her way.

Next she came upon warriors who were applying ochre to their bodies, and realising they had no fat, she said to them: "Hey you warriors, if you give me a necklace I will give you a piece of meat which you could use as fat". The warriors consented and gave her a necklace in exchange for the fat piece of meat. When the exchange was finalised, Hare took leave of the warriors and continued on her way.

Next she came upon Antelope to whom she said: "Look at my necklace". On enquiring where she had got it, Hare replied, "It is my friends the warriors who gave it to me, the warriors to whom I gave my meat, the meat the hunters gave me, the hunters to whom I gave my arrow, my arrow which my God gave me". Antelope looked at Hare's necklace admiringly and said: "May I please try it on?" On wearing the necklace Antelope sought the opinion of her friend by asking: "Does it suit me?" To this Hare innocently replied, "It suits you perfectly well". Thereupon Antelope ran as fast as her legs could carry her, running away

162

with Hare's beads. After trying to pursue Antelope, Hare soon realised that she would never catch up with her, and so gave up the chase.

Walking away sorrowfully, Hare soon came upon another group of hunters and said to them: "Hey you hunters, please shoot that antelope for me". To this the hunters asked: "What is she guilty of?" Hare replied: "She took away my necklace, my necklace which the warriors gave me, the warriors to whom I gave meat, my meat that the hunters gave me, the hunters to whom I gave my arrow, my arrow that my God gave me". After hearing of Hare's complaint, the hunters declined to shoot Antelope.

Taking leave of the hunters, Hare next came across a burning fire, to whom she said: "Hey you fire, could you please eat those hunters?" Fire asked: "What have they done?" Hare replied: "They refused to shoot Antelope, Antelope who took away my necklace, my necklace which the warriors gave me, the warriors to whom I gave meat, my meat that the hunters gave me, the hunters to whom I gave my arrow, my arrow that my God gave me". Again, on hearing Hare's complaint, Fire too said: "I will not eat the hunters".

Hare next came upon Water and said to it: "Hey you water, could you please put out that fire?" Water asked: "What has Fire done?" Hare repeated to Water all that she had told Fire. Water on listening to Hare's complaint declined to do as she was bid. Hare left Water feeling disappointed. Soon she found a herd of elephants to whom she spoke thus: "Hey you elephants, could you please drink that water?" On enquiring why water had to be drunk, Hare replied: "Water refused to put out Fire, Fire who refused to eat the hunters, the hunters that declined to shoot Antelope, Antelope who took away my necklace, my necklace which the warriors gave me, the warriors to whom I gave meat, my meat that the hunters gave me, the hunters to whom I gave my arrow, my arrow that my God gave me". On hearing Hare's story, the elephants declined to carry out Hare's request as all the others had done.

Undaunted by her inability to convince anyone to take action on her behalf, Hare moved on, next coming upon trees to whom she spoke, saying: "Hey you trees, could you please fall on those elephants?" On enquiring the wrong committed by the elephants, Hare replied: "They refused to drink Water, Water that refused to put out Fire, Fire that refused to eat the hunters, the hunters that declined to shoot Antelope, Antelope who took away my beads, my beads which the warriors gave me, the warriors to whom I gave meat, my meat that the hunters gave me, the hunters to whom I gave my arrow, my arrow that my God gave me". When the trees had heard Hare's story they too said, "We will not fall on the elephants". Hare then left the trees and came upon termites whom she asked to fell the trees. The termites demanded to know the wrong committed by the trees. Hare told the termites how the trees had refused to fall on the elephants and went on enumerating what everyone else had done or refused to do, in the same way she had told the others. The refusal by the termites to fell the trees upset Hare, but she was by no means daunted.

Moving on and persistently, Hare soon came upon donkeys whom she asked to trample on the termites. On learning what the termites had done, the donkeys too declined to trample on them.

By this time Hare was beginning to feel exasperated and weary, having walked all day with no success. It was not long before she came upon a group of hyenas, to whom she said: "Hey you hyenas could you please eat those donkeys?" The hyenas asked: "What have the donkeys done?" Hare replied, "They refused to trample on the termites, the termites which refused to fell the trees, the trees that refused to fall on the elephants, the elephants who refused to drink Water, Water who refused to put out Fire, Fire who refused to eat the hunters, the hunters who declined to shoot Antelope, Antelope who took away my necklace, my necklace which the warriors gave me, the warriors to whom I gave meat, my meat that the hunters gave me, the hunters to whom I gave my arrow, my arrow that God gave me". Agreeing to carry out Hare's requests, the hyenas said: "Very well we shall eat the donkeys".

On realisation that they were about to be eaten, the donkeys said: "We will trample on the termites". The termites said: "We will fell the trees". The trees said: "We will fall on the elephants". The elephants said: "We will drink Water." Water said: "I will put out Fire". Fire said: "I will eat the hunters". The hunters said: "We will shoot Antelope". Antelope said: "I will return Hare's necklace." So Hare was given back her necklace, and she was very happy. My story ends there.[32]

In this narrative one notices what may be called a 'build-up' plot. The protagonist undergoes cumulative experiences, gathering and trading objects and getting into a quagmire. Every time she comes across possible help she has to repeat the foregoing occurrences. At the end she comes across a charitable character who is ready to help.

There are other stories with 'build down' plots. In this case there is a reduction rather than an accumulation of issues. In one such Luo narrative, a girl and her brother go into the forest. The brother branches off to see a friend promising to join the sister in due course. The girl meets six ogres upon which she begins to sing calling her brother. The ogres listen and leave her unharmed. She continues to meet five, four, three, two and finally one ogre.

The last one swallows her. The brother also comes across the ogres. They sing to him that they have not eaten his sister and to the last ogre that Obong'o is on his way there. When Obong'o reaches it, the ogre refuses to let him pass upon which he gets ready to spear it. But it pleads and asks that its small finger be cut which leads to the retrieval of the sister and all other people the ogre had swallowed before.[33]

Both the build-up and build-down plots help to create suspense. In the foregoing story, the increasing number of unwilling animals make us wonder whether Hare would eventually get a helper. When that happens, we see a reversal of statements by all those who had refused to help. Using these techniques a narrator can easily shorten or lengthen a narrative.

The point about shortening or lengthening a narrative is explained by Finnegan in the following words:

> There is often no fixed wording, and the narrator is free to bind together the various episodes, motifs, characters and forms at his disposal into his own unique creation, suited to the audience, the occasion or the whims of the moment.[34]

This recognition gives us insight into the elasticity of the African narrative. It is not actually out of place to think of an African oral novel out of the various motifs and episodes that can be stringed into one long story. For example, the adventures of Hare can be a basis of such a story, as follows:

> Once Hare had many friends. One day he went to visit Dove. On that day, Dove had aired her crops to dry. The sky was heavy with clouds and soon it would start falling. Hare was worried about his friend's crops and panickingly started gathering them. But Dove was unperturbed. When it started falling, she simply sang and the crops stored themselves. The vain Hare blurted out: "Ah my friend! So you just do as I do? Come and visit me one day". When Dove went, Hare's song worked no miracles and his crops were rained on.
>
> He went on doing this kind of thing with other animals and losing their friendship. When he had lost all, he chanced on a spider who thought him a likable fellow. They became good friends and soon Spider invited him to a journey to go and woo in heaven. He spun his web and they were able to reach heaven. But while there, Hare started to play his tricks convincing Spider's bride that she would have a very hard time fetching water for Spider's many legs. The bride immediately decided to decline Spider. When Spider discovered that it was his friend that had discredited him, he folded his web and returned to Earth leaving Hare there. Unable to do anything, Hare decided to jump down to Earth. He fell until he thought he was never going to reach the ground. Then suddenly,

he crashed on the ground and instantly became a dry chunk of meat. A woman who was walking from her maiden home to her marital home chanced on this meat and picked it up as a surprise conciliatory gift to her husband. She put it in the basket she had on her head and in which she had also kept her child's food.

Once in the basket, the meat changed into Hare and started playing pranks on the baby strapped on the back of the woman. But every time the child complained, the mother scolded it for being ridiculous. At that time Hare changed back into meat. On reaching home the woman cut it up and prepared stew. Her husband was so happy that he invited other friends for a feast. But as soon as they gathered, Hare collected himself and dashed off spilling the soup into their faces. He also picked the child's shoes which he wore into the bush.

As he was strolling in the bush one day, he met Elephant who was so impressed that he asked Hare how he could get some shoes also. Hare assured him that he could make him some. He advised Elephant to collect firewood to make the shoes. After six days, there was an impressive heap of firewood ready.

Hare asked Elephant to climb onto the heap as he lit the fire. Elephant complained of the heat but Hare told him that if he did not want the shoes then he could leave but had to pay for wasting Hare's time. Elephant endured but in the end collapsed and died.

Hare bored a hole into his intestines from where he collected blubber for his porridge: He kept it a secret from his sister who always wondered why Hare's porridge was so sweet. One day the sister followed and saw him enter elephant's stomach. She blocked his passage with cow dung and he pleaded for so long before she released him. On coming out, he abused her in the vilest language and they parted company.

The animals of the jungle found their king dead and a meeting was called to find the killer. They contacted a medicineman who divined that the killer was a small hornless animal. They decided to hunt for him in vain. Later another meeting was called for all horned animals to chart out a strategy of netting the murderer.

Hare heard of the meeting and was curious to know the agenda. He asked his wife to bring the horns hanging on the walls and wax them onto his head as horns. She initially declined but yielded when he threatened to beat her up although she advised him to avoid sitting in the sun where the heat would melt the wax.

As soon as Hare strode into the meeting arena, he headed straight for the dais in the hot sun. No sooner had the discussions caught heat than his horns tumbled

166

down from his head. The other animals immediately dashed for him as the killer of their king. But he manoeuvred his way and escaped.

He hid for a long time until he could hide no longer. So he decided to challenge Elephant's successor to a fight to determine the rightful king. Seeing this as a chance to net him, Lion readily agreed to the duel and a date was set. Lion rallied all the big guns to cheer him tearing Hare to pieces while Hare came alone with the small animals too scared to side with him. He only carried three gourds – one containing red paint, another porridge and the third bees.

When the fight started, he took the first gourd and hit it on Lion's head. The animals saw the red paint which they believed to be blood. The king was in trouble. Hare added the second and they saw porridge as Lion's brains. Unable to stand it any longer they started warning Lion that he was facing death. The third gourd landed releasing the swarm of bees. They bit the animals and gave Lion a chase of his life. Lion ran and only saved himself by jumping into a well. But even then, the bees kept buzzing there for further assault. He stayed there and eventually drowned.

Hare became the king and the other animals started sending him presents like dried meat which he fed to his visitors. One time zebra visited him and wondered where he got such nice meat. Hare told him that there was a forest from where he gathered it. So they arranged for a trip there.

On the appointed day, he led Zebra to the foot of a rocky hill and told him to lie down as he climbed to go and roll the meat down. Zebra had to close his eyes as soon as he heard a crashing sound as that would be the meat rolling down. Very determined to get the meat, Zebra faithfully followed the instructions. Hare went and rolled a big boulder which came tumbling down and killing Zebra instantly. He skinned Zebra and kept the meat.

He did this with many animals until he met Leopard. Having been impressed with Hare's meat, he also asked to be taken to the forest of meat. But he suspected foul play and did not close his eyes. So when Hare rolled the stone, he moved aside and saved himself. He lay prostrate feigning death. Hare gathered his 'meat' and put it into the basket for the journey home strapping it on his back. As they went on Leopard extended his paw and pricked Hare's head. Sensing danger, Hare threw down the basket and escaped. Leopard gave a chase but did not catch him. So he went to wait for him in the lair.

Hare returned at night sensing danger, started knocking on the door shouting, "Hodi, my house". There was no reply. Hare went on, "Hodi, my house. What is wrong today? Every day I call to my house and it replies welcoming me home".

167

He knocked again, "Hodi, my house". Leopard gruffly answered, "Come in Sir". Hare had of course found out what he wanted and dashed off saying, "Since when did I hear a house speaking?"

And one can go on linking these stories. The above brief account is a summary of what exist as eight independent stories but the character of which make them combineable into a 'novel'. This elasticity gives leeway to the narrators's creativity and flexibility. It is actually the base of what have been recorded as epics in the form of published texts like *Sundiata: An Epic of Old Mali, Emperor Shaka the Great* e.t.c.

It would be incomplete discussing the structure of narratives without mentioning the characteristic beginnings and endings. Most narratives begin with statements like: "Long time ago...", "Once upon a time...", "In the olden days..." e.t.c. Because of the recurrence of these phrases in many narratives, they are recognised also as formulas, in this case, internal formulas. These initial statements can be termed 'Opening internal formulas'. and this counterparts the "Closing internal formulas" e.g. "They lived happily ever after...", "That is why this and that happens...", "And that is the origin of the proverb..." e.t.c.

Setting

Setting is the location of the events and characters in a story. It can be seen in three dimensions viz: time (historical), place (geographical) and situation (sociological). Timewise the oral narratives are always set in past as indicated by the internal formulas as "Once upon a time", "In the olden days", etc. The historical setting is a safety valve for the narrator as it indicates the impression that he is not really talking about the present and no one can accuse him of slander. It also gives the narrative fictionality. The events do not have to have happened and even if they did, the narrator is not tied down to being exactly factual. The lapse of time that has purportedly passed is an excuse for the various distortions and incredibilities that may be in the story.

Place setting is the geographical location of the action. It can be a village, forest, the sky, anywhere. Usually, the place is not explicitly mentioned, but it unfolds itself automatically. The actual name of the place may not be there but it is tacitly understood by the audience that these things took place in their community and hence at the place their forefathers inhabited. In the course of the narrative the place setting may change several times due to the movement of characters and the events. For example, a story may start off in a **village** with several suitors coming for a beautiful girl who is too proud and fastidious. It then moves to a **dance arena** where a transmuted ogre wins her heart. Together they walk home along a **path** up to the ogre's home. After discovering her mistake, she escapes into the **bush** and runs to a **riverbank** where a benevolent frog swallows her and wades across to land her safely on the **other bank**, her gateway to safety. Then she travels back to her **village**. In this instance, the setting has changed from the village, the dance arena, the path to the ogre's home, the bush, the riverbank, the frog's stomach, the river and finally the village. It is like a motion picture.

Sociological setting refers to the social situations, political relationships and economic issues in the community where the story takes place. For example there may be tranquility, strong friendship, a love affair, a famine, a dance, war e.t.c. As with the physical setting, there are progressive changes in the sociological setting as the story develops. In a famous Luo story, for example, a man Nyamgondho, starts off in abject poverty. Then there is a windfall of wealth from a mysterious being he fishes from the lake. He becomes wealthy and arrogant. This leads him to insulting the mysterious woman who then departs with all her wealth putting him into total humiliation and even physical dissipation.

Some settings are credible in that they are recognisable and real. But often the settings are incredible and are just actually imaginative creations. Something like a host of hyenas hanging on the hawk's tail for a flight to the sky is such a fantasy. Fantastic settings and events are used for graphical and symbolic purposes. When we see the hawk flying higher into the sky, we inevitably see the stupidity of the hyenas and are suspended as we expect the great fall.

The graphic impressions created by use of words is technically called imagery. The images may be classified according to the senses to which they appeal viz: olfactory (smell senses), visual (sight), tactile (touch), audial (hearing) and apical (taste).

Most times images are used in narratives to stand for wider ideas. A putrefying carcass for example, could stand for degradation and disintegration morally. A grotesque ogre stands for vice and death. The representation of larger ideas by images is called "symbolism" and the images are then symbols. Like the frog that swallows the bride to safety is a symbol of benevolence and security.

Characters

A character is a being involved in the events of a story. It may be human, animal, object or spirit. The range of characters include people, animals, stones, trees, plants, deities, spirit, ogres, birds, e.t.c. The narrative characters are often symbolic. Thus there are certain recurrent patterns of behaviour identified with specific characters e.g. Hare – trickery, Tortoise – wisdom, Elephant – nobility, Hyena – gluttony, Ogre – malice, e.t.c. When a character repeatedly appears in more or less the same role he becomes a "stock character". But this does not mean that the same characters do not appear in other roles. In these characters we actually see ourselves since they are but masks. In the narratives we can identify the gossip, interloper, glutton, braggart, opportunist, laggard, activist, agitator, e.t.c. They are usually presented with exaggerated sharpness to emphasise the idiosyncrasies. Use of exaggeration is called "Hyperbole" or "Caricaturing" especially if it is meant to ridicule. The exposure to ridicule is called "Satire". These are important elements for conveyance of messages.

In a clearer pursuit of characterology, the next sub-section is a look at two categories of characters – the Ogre to represent the malignant and birds to represent the benign.

The Ogre Character

The Ogre is a fantastic grotesque monster that appears in oral narratives often in contests of life and death with man. He is characterised by extremes of physical form and behaviour. Conceptually, the ogre is neither human nor animal but displays characteristics of both. We will look at his configuration in Luo, Maasai and Gikuyu narratives.

The Luo ogre is generically called Apul Apul or Opul Opul, the former name being the more common. Other brand names include Kaki, Otoyo (Hyena) and Ondiek (beast). Thus we can generally conclude that he belongs to the fraternity of beasts.

Impliedly the ogre is male but he is able to transform into a beautiful female to beguile an unsuspecting male. In one narrative the ogre comes to a village dance to trace the cutter of its tail. He changes into the prettiest girl and demands that each player declaim his praise name to win "her". "She" declines all except the one who brags of being the cutter of the ogre's tail. The ogre readily agrees to accompany him home. At night the ogre becomes itself and attempts to devour Obon'go except for the prompt intervention of his dogs. The struggle goes on until morning when the "girl" requests her lover to go and get dry firewood from the forest to warm themselves the next night. The dogs are locked away. The bush trip gives it an opportunity to revenge. As soon as Obon'go is atop the tree, the Ogre becomes itself and begins cutting the tree. Eventually, some doves intervene and save Obon'go.[35]

As it were, the ogre is very schematic and vengeful. Notice the clever scheme of locking the dogs from accompanying them to the bush. The stock way of having its revenge is by eating the victims or killing them. The ogre seems to have an abysmal stomach as it can swallow even whole villages. This quality is fantasised even more when we realise that the victims are preserved in the stomach and usually retrieved in the end by cutting the little finger. The fact of eating people makes the ogre a cannibal. But it not only eats people, it also eats of its own kind, hence is a double cannibal.

The schematism and complicity of the ogre is the best demonstrated in the Luo story of "Obwanda and the Hyena". In this story, the ogre conspires with Obwanda's lover that he, the ogre, can disguise himself and get the girl for the admirer. So he goes to a

170

medicineman to treat his gruff voice and enable him to sing like the girl's mother. He is instructed not to eat beetles on the way or stop to admire dancing star grass. But the ogre is so gullible that he fails to resist these temptations. The most outstanding thing is, however his determination to achieve the goal. So he keeps going back to the medicineman.[36] In another version of the same story, the medicineman has to tie his eyes with blinkers.

The ogre is not a trustworthy fellow. In the complicity with Obwanda's admirer, he turns round and wants the girl for himself. Thus he betrays their contract. In simple terms, he is very selfish and greedy.

And quite a bully he is also. With his monstrous size and grotesque body, he easily threatens and intimidates. In the Obon'go story, the ogre cuts the trees as he says: "You shit, you are the one who cut my tail and you are going to pay for it". When interfered with by the doves, he curses: "Stupid busybody, why didn't you interfere when my tail was being stolen?"

In another story where he chases the escaping girls and finds a distended tortoise which he suspects of hiding the girls, he threatens it with a beating saying: "Alright, I shall take you and dash you on this rock and burst you open". When the tortoise tricks him into dashing it into the water instead, his inanity is exposed. In another instance, this stupidity is shown when he labours to carry water in a wicker basket without realising the futility of that attempt.

Although the ogre generally cuts a despicable figure, it occasionally appears in a positive light. When this happens, it is meant to emphasise the vice of man. For example, in one story the ogre catches a woman and her grandchild red-handed stealing his crops. We would expect him to swallow them instantly. But no, he acts judiciously and strikes a bargain with them: "I've caught you stealing my potatoes... but I am prepared to make a bargain with you. You and I will wrestle. If you throw me, you will take all the potatoes you've dug. If I manage to throw you, then I shall simply eat you"[38].

Such instances are exceptions rather than the order. It is therefore rational to conclude that the Luo ogre is an agent of vice and malevolent forces that act against man's prosperity. These vices often appear to triumph over man but only for a season. Just as the valiant fighters overcome the ogre, so is man a relentless fighter in the face of vice and malice.

The Gikuyu ogre shares many of the characteristics with the Luo ogre. But the Gikuyu ogre's configuration often includes being hairy and having two mouths – one at the back and one in front. It is able to disguise itself as a handsome man and trick naive girls.

In many tales, he is very taunting and sadistic. In a story, "The Ogre and the Girl"[39], he asks for a woman's fingers and eats them one by one, oblivious of the pain it causes the victim. Also in "The New Mother", it teases and starves the newly delivered mother.

The ogre is also very conceited and grandiose. He is so full of himself and glees in mirth and arrogance. This forgetful grandiosity undoes it as it blurs his perception and sensitivity to his vocation. In the story "Mukuru Muriati's Niece"[40], the ogre has successfully disguised himself and so far enjoyed the hospitality accorded to the "niece". But he falters when given the task of guarding the garden. While the genuine niece, hitherto being mistreated, actively scares away the birds, the ogre throws out the crops to the monkeys thus he is discovered and arraigned.

The Maasai ogre is also grotesque. In "The Warrior with Two Mouths"[41], he has two mouths and very long hair. He also has the ability to change into a handsome young man. We get this impression from a story about a crow who is actually an ogre who wants to marry the village beauty.[42]

The Maasai ogre is also a man-eater as well as an eater of its own kind. He either swallows whole and raw or roasts before eating. The last feature makes the ogre more like human beings. In the story, "The Girl Who Married A Crow", the crow lights a big fire to roast before eating her. In "A Young Woman and an Ogre"[43], the ogre wants to eat her ceremoniously by laying her on prestigious leaves. So she takes him through the forest hunting for the ideal leaves but this is only her delaying tactic until her lover appears and kills the ogre.

This ceremoniousness in the Maasai ogre gives us his other quality of grandiosity and hedonism. He enjoys pleasurable things. In yet another story, "Mbiti"[44], the horde of ogres that have come to feast on Mbiti's visitor make a big bonfire to warm themselves. But this hedonism is laced with sadism and fervent greed. In "Mbiti", the ogre has a very crude way of testing whether the girl is ready for eating after fattening her. "And whenever Mbiti wanted to check how fat the girl had grown, she would prick her with a needle and when she complained of this treatment, Mbiti would comfort her saying: 'Oh, I didn't mean to do it my child'" And when the group of ogres wait in vain for the feast, they angrily burst into the hut and tear Mbiti to pieces.

The ogres live as human beings do, a fact which emphasises that they are but masks of humanity. They keep cattle, get children, stay in homes and express love. In "Konyek"[45], the ogre marries a human bride and gets a baby-boy. The husband ogre is so intimate with the wife that he admonishes the inquisitive son when the latter suspects some intrigue being played by his mother.

This same story gives us a very intelligent ogre in the child. First of all, he is the one who notices the woman hiding on top of the tree in the bush. He later questions the shrivelled rats the mother gives him purporting them to be the twins from the woman's womb. He also notices the footmarks of the children and expresses his concern but is overruled by the father's admonitions. Tired of him, the father grabs and swallows him. But he slithers through the anus to the father's discomfiture. In the end when the grown children kill them, he regretfully tells the father that his sensitivity could have saved them.

Using the notes from the three communities, we can generalise about the ogre. In fact the characteristics noted seem to recur with only slight variations. The ogre is generally a monstrous and grotesque creature who may be hairy, have two mouths, emit fire, is insatiable and can eat a lot of food and even people or objects like spears and utensils. He has an amorphous physiology, being able to change into different things for purposes of disarming his victims.

He is not physically attractive by any standards. He is in fact threatening and frightful. He is not different from those in society who specialise in ugly deeds but who can appear very mild and sociable to gain access to the victims. This is the category of drug traffickers, smugglers, master con-men, e.t.c. They operate from their hideouts from where they launch lethal attacks on the tranquil society. But as always happens, their numbered days always come to an end and they get netted and ejected. The finale is their succumbing to the power of law and justice represented by the ogre surrendering his finger to be cut to take out his victims.

The ogre is cruel, malicious and sadistic. He always schemes to cause chaos to man and relishes when there is suffering. If and when he gets the opportunity to taunt man, he does it to the maximum without as much as blinking an eyelid. But he is an avowed coward who shrinks at the slightest indication of danger. Whatever impudence and defiance he shows is an outward fabrication to keep appearing strong. He is a liar, betrayer, thief, conspirant, intimidator and dictator. His entry into a tranquil society causes immediate disequilibrium. He is in fact the epitome of disability. He descends on humanity with the gusto of military coup leaders and wrecks similar havoc.

What makes him such a malignant force is the importunity with which he pursues his vocations. Beaten once, he never gives up and keeps revising his strategy until he achieves success. But the success is very temporal since he is gullible and has strong personal weaknesses. One of these is forgetfulness. Many times he displays this by say, eating up the utensils at the home where he is a suitor, or leaving his compound littered with tale-telling bones. This constitutes a tragic flaw which leads to his being found out and dealt with.

He is inane, lacks foresight and lives for the moment forgetting that fortunes change. Thus he is easily duped and trapped. In all contests with man, he is the perennial loser, except in very few cases.

In general, the character stands for evil and death. He symbolises the ominous flail of vice looming over humanity and threatening to reduce it to nothingness. He is a replica of those of us who are dehumanised, alienated, immoral and egotistically ready to achieve their goals by hook or crook and regardless of the repercussions on the larger society. They exist in all sectors of society; ubiquity is their trademark. And when we encounter them in real life or in fiction, they are an adventurous picture. Their final defeat accords us a catharsis of sorts. But only for a while for there seems to be an interminable struggle, a vicious cycle.

Bird Characters

Birds are ecological factors in our environment. As it were, their existence in our tropical climate is taken for granted such that we rarely stop to think what the atmosphere would be like without them. The sight of flying or perching birds is visually stimulating. This sight is augmented by the music they produce. They herald our mornings and coo the eves away. In simple terms, their euphony is aesthetic and any sensitive being emotionally appreciates.

Human societies regard different birds with different beliefs. Some are seen as signs of bad omen while others are the opposite or some other thing. The Maasai initiands for instance have to go shooting down birds to be dried in readiness for the lifetime ceremony of circumcision. The Luo see the vulture as a sign of death and the dove as a graceful bird. The Turkana see the Nightjar as a sign of rain.[46]

The dove universally seems to be a bird of good fortune. Reading through the biblical story of Noah's Ark, the dove is the bird that is sent to check on the water level. In today's world it is one of the most commonly domesticated birds. It seems to be inextricably related to men.

Oral narratives have many bird characters: magpies, sparrows, parrots, crows, vultures and a host of others. With a few exceptions, birds have to always play a positive role in resolving conflicts and salvaging protagonists. They are personified and made to play larger than animal roles. The next few pages contain a kind of taxonomy of the roles of birds in oral narratives.

Birds seem to always appear at times of crisis. By some stroke of good luck or fate, when the protagonist is in dire trouble, a bird or swarm of them appears on the scene and opens up possibilities of salvation. In the story, "The New Mother", birds appear and resurrect the hopes of contact between the woman and her husband in the forest. The woman muses at their appearance: "Oh dear, these little birds if I would but send them to my husband since he went and will find me eaten by the ogres". So she sends them to deliver her message. The birds act as emissaries of urgent and important messages. They convey information about the suffering or imminent death of the protagonist. Symbolically, they are a bridge between the two spheres of action. While the woman is unable to walk to the forest or even shout and be heard, the birds can fly there.

174

And birds are able to do these duties with maximum invincibility, being in the air and out of reach of the antagonists. The most the latter can do is to scare them away with stones, sticks or noise which is not a permanent solution. We get this impression in a Luo story, "The Four Sons"[47] when the ogre is chasing away the birds and cursing. He "ran frantically to and fro, snapping at the air", but the birds kept returning and in the end the ogre cannot fully cut the tree and kill Obon'go.

The birds undertake their vocation with a lot of importunity. However much they are chased, they return and repeat their message. In "The New Mother", it is even ironical that it is the smiths that send away the birds until the importunity cues them that there could be something amiss. The persistence of the protagonist birds parallels that of the evil ogres.

The role of the birds is however not restricted to relaying messages. They also counsel the protagonists. In "The Four Sons" the doves advise Obong'o to call the dogs. And again they do not just do the service for nothing. There is a reciprocation. Sometimes they actually strike a bargain but at other times they benefit from the gratitude of their beneficiaries. The rewards could be cattle, grains, blood or some fitting prize.

The four points of importunity, delivery of messages, counselling and bargaining are explicit in the extract below from the Maasai story "Mbiti".

> One day Mbiti went to invite her friends to come and feast on the girl. But while she was away, a crow went to visit the girl. She found her tanning a hide discarding the fleshy parts of it. He said to her: "If you give me one of those strips I will tell you something nice" **(bargain-sic)**. The girl said to the crow, "Get away, you have nothing to tell me!" She threw a stone at him in a bid to chase him away. The crow circled the area and reappeared from another direction. He again begged the girl for a fleshy strip of hide promising to tell her something **(importunity-sic)**. The girl eventually grew impatient with the bird, and she angrily threw a strip of hide at him, saying as she did so: "There you go, you glutton, though you have nothing to tell me". When the crow had eaten, he said to the girl: "You know, Mbiti went to fetch some other animals to come and feast on you **(relaying information)**. So you had better apply ashes to your body and go as quickly as you can back to your home, and if the monsters ask you who you are, you must answer: "I am only a wandering skin of ashes" **(advice and counsel-sic)**.[48]

As far as relaying of messages is concerned, the speech abilities of birds is brought into focus. We know that birds do not generally speak. But from linguistic studies we know that they communicate among themselves using sounds which can be decoded into mating sounds, fright sounds, e.t.c. The parrots, though, have some rudimentary speech abilities and are able to imitate and reproduce practised human sounds and words. It is not surprising that in one Luo narrative a parrot reveals the identity of a killer[49]. The possession of these speech abilities, sketchy though they are, underscores their credibility as message carriers. We note that in one Maasai narrative, "The Warrior and Dove"[50], all animals that come to be sent are inarticulate except the dove whose fluency impresses. The jackal says it would relay the message "Wua, wua" and the hyena"Uuu, uuu". They don't even stop to inquire about the details of the warrior sending them. The Dove on the other hand starts by asking: "Tell me what your name is first, then I will know what to say." After getting that information, Dove inquires about the location of the village and the mother's hut. Then she says she would sing:

> Father of Loolmon'i-wuasin
> Mother of Loolmon'gi-wuasin,
> Loolmon'gi-wuasin is at Kerikere well
> Eight straps
> Eight straps.

This convinces the warrior of the dove's competence to do the duty. The sensibility and candour comes out again in birds as moral voices. They confront and nag the evil-doers until justice is done. In a Gikuyu tale, "The Woman and the Bird"[51], a bird whose eggs have been crushed by a woman complains and promises retribution in the following words:

> You have killed my children, haven't you?
> You will cry from sunset to sunset.

When it eventually gets even with the woman by eating her child, it says:

> Do not weep, that is how you killed my children
> This time it is me who killed your child.

Thus it emphasises an important environmental point that life is just as precious to the other animals as it is to the human being. We have no choice but to embrace the Bird's retribution.

By such actions the birds reveal to us the fallacies in man. In certain cases they actually test some virtues like patience and tolerance. In a Gikuyu story, "Thiiru the Medicineman"[52], a bird goes clearing the remaining patches in the man's farm. The man considers it a god-send until the harvesting time comes when the bird also continues to reap to the man's ire. Thiiru traps the bird and charges it with stealing. The bird's defence is that it was only taking its fair share from its contribution in the cultivation.

In a more or less similar story from the Luo, the bird plants weeds on the patches cultivated by the woman. She traps and gives it out as a present to her son Owuor. The next day she discovers that the bird has filled the pot of confinement with grains. She puts the magic bird into more pots and becomes rich overnight. The bird in this case is a symbol of fatalistic benevolence. This motif continues throughout the story until later when the boy lets it escape. The father is so annoyed that he takes the boy and abandons him in the forest. But again it is the bird that changes into a handsome young man and rescues the boy. We can see a neat parallel here between the transformation of the bird and that of the ogres, one for positive reasons and the other for the reverse.

In summary then, the birds can be seen as guardians of life. They do all that goes to preserve life in a majority of cases. In one Gikuyu narrative, the dove actually resurrects a cadaver three times. The story goes:

The Life-giving Dove

A long time ago there was a man and his wife. They had a girl. This girl fell sick many times. She died. When she died, she was thrown away and a dove came and put her together again. The dove took the girl to a cave where she lived. But after a short while the girl said that she wanted to go back to her mother. The dove told the girl that she must stay in the cave, but still the girl went. Now when she went home, she fell sick again. She died and she was thrown away again. The dove came, put her together and took her away. But the girl went home again intending never to return to the cave. Now when the dove came to fetch her, she stood outside and sang:

> Uu ai uuai! Give me my ornament give me back
> Then I can go back home where the rain comes down
> With ta, ta, ta.

The parents closed the door but they forgot to close the window and so the dove slipped in through the window and went straight where the girl was sleeping. She took away what she had given to the girl and the girl was all bones again. These bones were thrown away and as usual the dove found them and put them together. She took the girl to a very far place and they lived there forever.[53]

Interfluence of Forms

This expression, borrowed from Austin Bukenya, means the blending or integration of different genres into one oral performance. In narratives, this mainly occurs in three forms.

(i) Use of dialogue (ii) Use of song (iii) Use of proverbs

Use of Dialogue

Dialogue is the verbal communication or conversation among or between characters. It is recognised as a stylistic aspect in that a narrative may as well be told as a report without verbatim reproduction of actual speech.

Characters do communicate by sounds or words. The non-human characters are personified and lent speech. The rendering of the speech to the audience creates a sense of realism and brings out the characters as live interactive agents. Dialogue makes them credible. Moreso we do not only analyse a character from what he says or does alone but also what the others say about him. These perceptions can be abstracted from the speeches.

Dialogue is one way through which the narrator enthuses his audience. Each character is presented with his idiosyncrasies by being mimicked in terms of speech defects, voice pitch and such other speech variations. This creates variety and makes both the narrative and the whole performance dramatic.

Use of Song

This is even more significant and widespread. Although not all narratives are interspersed with songs, a good number are. The songs within the stories play both a thematic and stylistic role. Below are some analytical points about the use of songs as style in narratives:

Episodic Division: The plot of narratives is such that there is a logical development of causes and effects in the progression of events. The episodes present important stages in the development of the narrative. Songs are used to divide these episodes and act as transitional points, structurally speaking. Thus after one episode, when a song comes in, the audience expects a movement of another happening. We get a very good example from a Gikuyu story about a girl ordained to die to allay a drought.[54] She has to be swallowed by the Earth in an open ground. As soon as she is stationed in the field, she sings questioning her condemnation:

And my own mother, do you say that I should get finished?
Mv own father, do you say that I should get finished?
My junior mother...
My junior father...
Kararu's daughter, I am condemned by fate
The rains will fall and I will get finished

The story goes on: "She started to sink into the ground. She sang again: (same song)." Her feet sink, followed by the legs, knees, waist, breasts until the whole body goes. At each stage she sings her song.

178

By dividing the episodes, the songs contribute to plot development and represent the passage of time. The audience is also kept in anticipation of the finale as the songs lengthen the narratives.

Theme Revelation: Thematically speaking, songs are very cogent summaries of narrative concerns. In the same story referred to in the foregoing pages, the girl talks about her fate and why it has to be so. The crux of the matter is that the society has to survive and that, by the falling of rain. An individual is sacrificed for the sakę of the many. She expresses the helplessness of her parents and relatives who wish to have her alive but are over-ruled by the oracle.

The songs even act as moral statements. We have an example in a Luo story where Obon'go is overcome by incestuous lust for his sister Awuor. He has carnal knowledge of her and is unable to withdraw after the act. In shame the defiled girl laments and condemns the act:

> Look at this mortal crime
> Committed by a wretch who calls himself my brother
> He rejects betrothal, because he needs only me, his sister
> Is this really me or another
> Whose virginity has been stolen so wickedly,
> and by the son of my father and mother?
> Obon'go burns for his sister Awuor.
> Pity of pities
> I'll see him burning like a torch flung on a bonfire.[55]

This song reveals the abnormality of Obon'go's act; he is blinded by lust and ignores the morally sanctioned betrothal. He has degraded his sister and robbed her of her pride. The song also gives the traditional penalty for the crime: cremation alive. The society has to preserve its dignity by getting rid of such vile offenders.

That is theme at the ideational level. Songs also give us emotional themes. The words and tunes portray the moods of the moment. The songs usually come at points of crisis. It is the duty of the narrator to create the intensity of the moment through the song.

Inter-character Communication: Quite often in narratives, characters communicate in song instead of dialogue. For example, in a story already referred to from the Luo, Owuor asks the fleeing birds to return by singing:

> Our bird, our bird
> which produces grain,
> please come back.

The bird sings back teasingly:

> Sicho, sicho your mother's madness
> which made
> her catch me and confine me.
> Sicho, sicho your mother's madness
> which made
> her catch and confine me.

Later when the father abandons him in the forest, he calls for the bird's help singing:

> Baba, you have truly left me
> Stranded in the jungle,
> Tutu the bird, I helped you
> Why don't you rescue me?[56]

At times the musical communication is a code meant to be understood by only the desired recipients. This is spotted in the Maasai narrative in which a girl has been captured by the ogre and she sings to call for her lover's help. She postpones her death by singing to the ogre not to eat her yet:

> Not here my bead
> Let us go to the water hole
> Where you can eat me
> And have a drink
> Oh my dear warrior, where was it?[57]

She flatters the ogre by calling him 'My bead' (The statement is rather ironical since it is her human lover that is her 'bead'). The secret code comes in the last line, "Oh my dear warrior, where was it?" She is asking the lover where it was they were supposed to meet as she has lost her way. The ogre is unable to decode the message and glees in the belief that he is being praised.

In many other cases, the song is monological and is for intra-character communication. It offers company and deters loneliness. It is also a spontaneous expression of emotion be it of joy, sadness, despair, e.t.c.

Aesthetic Enhancement: Song somewhat has a stronger appeal to emotion than speech. The use of song adds the musical dimension to narratives and by that enhance their beauty. In fact some narratives have so much song in them that they qualify to be called 'musical narratives'. Here is an example, from the Maasai.

Hyena and Cow

Once upon a time a cow strayed and could not find her way home. Three days passed before she was found. On the third day she went to the river for a drink of water. At the river she came upon a hyena to whom she sang:

> I beg you please le uu
> I am the cow with a suckling calf
> This is my third day without
> a drink
> And the December sun has made me thirsty.

Hyena answered:

> It is rather too late (swearing)
> First I will suffocate you with my smell
> Then I will rip off the roots of your udder
> Next I will make you squat like a constipated bitch.

> There is nothing that does not come to an end
> Our feasting on the brown Ole Wuargas has ended
> The one who is felled by the bell as we chase
> As we chase, as we chase:

> What is heard in that bush saying Kau!
> It is the large eater with blade-shaped ears
> He that carries food until he is overcome
> Yet he does not share it with his poor mother
> He came and he tripped near the stomach
> And with his mouth he pressed against a rotten spleen

> Oh sister who has gone visiting other villages
> As you fence the homestead, do so but remember me

> Remember your brother who is yet to come
> For fencing use dry straw
> The ones that I would simply push aside with the tongue
> As I the bull walk in.

> A suckling cow satisfies not the limper
> Twenty sheep are but a speck between the teeth
> An ox with a bell is pure starvation.

Hoe hoo I swear.

When the hyena had sang to the cow, he swore, laughed and ate her up. And that is the end.[58]

(Notes: 1. Le uu is an onomatopoeic name for Hyena.

2. Ole Wuargas refers to an ox).

Use of Proverbs

More often, proverbs are found in narratives at the end, summarising the theme or moral lesson. This consolidates the morals.

However, not all narratives end or have to end in proverbs. When they do the point is worth noting. The interfluence can be appreciated from two views. One is that the proverbs arise out of the narratives e.g. a Maasai story ends: "From this story there originates the saying: 'The ostrich cannot be deprived of her feathers'[59]. On the other plane the narratives can be seen as illustrations of the proverbs. Thus a narrative may be titled with a proverb which the story illustrates. Both ways the proverb and the narrative come together.

SOCIAL FUNCTIONS OF NARRATIVES

Socialisation

The telling of and listening of stories is a social activity that brings people together to share in an artistic and creative affair. The occasion is meant to entertain. The fictionality of the narratives transposes the participants into a world of imagination and for a while they forget the drudgery of daily life. They are transplanted to a world of make-believe. As the narrator goes through the nuances of recreating the fictional world, the audience is carried along like passengers on a flight. They, at that time do everything as if the story is true. To augment the story is the narrator's creativity and dramatic impact, especially when mimicking the characters. The success with which he does this enthuses the audience in varying degrees and affords them relaxation through laughter and purgation of pent-up emotions as they go through the undulations of the moments.

The enjoyment derived is facilitated by the social organisation of the participants. The atmosphere is generally an informal one with no coercion or harassment. Everyone there is on equal footing with the colleagues be he male, female, child or adult. There is no discrimination and the participation is democratic. Each participant has a chance to narrate and listen. And because no one wants to let the group down or embarrass himself, there is an intrinsic motivation to always have a story to tell. The emphasis is on voluntary rather than mandatory participation. The situation underscores the value of social co-operation.

In any social activity that brings a group together, discipline is paramount. The narrative occasion instills discipline inductively. This is first because one goes to the occasion voluntarily and with a tacit agreement to adhere to the conventions prevailing. He has to observe the procedure being followed and exercise both restraint and patience. One mark of the discipline is to let the narrator have the silence and time to go through, however uninteresting the tale may be. If one feels bored, he waits for his turn to tell a more lively tale or hear one from another person.

The discipline inherent in the narration is inevitably transferred to other spheres of life. The person learns to respect others, appreciate personal differences in abilities and temperament and be able to relate in a common activity.

Most important is that the narration enables people to spend their leisure time usefully instead of idling and probably engaging in undesirable activities.

Mental Stimulation.

The human being has five senses – that of sight, smell, hearing, taste and touch. By nervous connection, these senses are connected to the brain, the single most important organ in the physical, mental and affective functioning of the person. Narratives are told and received through the ear. The information is then transferred to the brain for interpretation, analysis and synthesis. This leads to a perception of the ideas and exhibition of reaction e.g. laughter, fright, depression, e.t.c.

The narrator must be of a cordinated mind so as to relate the tale logically from the beginning to the end. A narrative consists of several episodes which relate to each other in a comprehensive sequence. It is requisite that the narrator maintains the order of events to achieve the organic unity and communicate with his audience. The logical rendition of the story makes it not only easy to understand but also to learn and retell. Even when a narrator varies the plot, he does it skilfully to maintain credibility.

The traditional oral narration occasion only demands the presence of the person with his auditory facilities. The demand it places on the narrator is to remember the story and tell it for a possible retelling in future. This is very good training for the memory. One has to be attentive to get the essentials of the story and assimilate it into his repertoire. The mind must therefore be very active to accommodate the new knowledge or varieties of what is already known.

As well as training of memory, the narratives also sharpen critical appreciation. One has to ingest the messages of the narratives, and evaluate the events related. In fact some narratives even demand a judgement of the happenings. The listener turns the events in his mind and debates on whether the course of events could have been different. He also relates the story vicariously to the present life. All these are mental activities.

Didactism

Functionalists have always emphasised the instructive roles of Orature. More than anything else they have recognised that narratives are not just told for their own sake but have some important pieces of social instruction to impart. This constitutes the didactic import of the narratives.

The allegories of events and characters reflect on human life and are a sourse of learning. In the characters, be they animal or otherwise, we see the lazy, sages, cowards, agitators, the arrogant e.t.c. And the tale gives us hints as to how to react to them.

From the narrative content, it is not difficult to understand what kind of audience a narrative is meant for, although to a great extent, most narratives could be relevant to the whole society. Even if that may be so, the tales may mean more to some groups than to others. For example there are tales targeted at the adolescents, maidens, warriors, clan elders, e.t.c.

The aim of didactism is to discourage vice and encourage virtue. The narratives give us guidelines on what is despicable and what is cherishable. In other words they seek to change life. To concretise our discussion, here is a tale from the Luo which makes a didactic point about the choice of marriage partners:

> Once upon a time there was an old squirrel and his son. The son had already passed the marriage age and the father was getting worried. So one day he summoned the son and asked him:
>
> 'Son you are now mature enough to get married. I do not have long to live and it would be my pleasure to depart after you are married. Why don't you get a girl to marry?'
>
> The son replied: 'Father, I agree with you and I have actually thought about marriage. In the first place I wanted to marry Tortoise's daughter. She is very intelligent and alert'.
>
> 'Why didn't you propose to her?' the father asked.
>
> 'Well she is a notorious gossip and I thought she could generate a lot of misunderstanding between me and clansmen'.
>
> 'That is true son', the father agreed.
>
> 'After that, I considered the snake's daughter. But she is very extravagant.

She needs so many new clothes and as I am not very rich, I may be tempted to steal to satisfy her demand for clothes', the son declared.

'Very correct. You have done well to discount her'.

'Then the daughter of the wild dog came into my mind. But then I saw that this family is very hot-tempered and I do not want to spend the rest of my life in noisy quarrels'.

'I once again see your point son, hot temper is a real problem that could cause more than what is foreseeable'.

'Having thus failed to settle on the nearby families, I began to nurse thoughts about the Hippo's daughter. But she is dull-witted and spends all the time eating and getting obese. I do not want a clumsy wife'.

The attentive father once again agreed with the son.

'Lastly, my dear father, I settled on Hyena's daughters. But it seems all of them in that family are thieves and gluttons. So I am still looking for a suitable wife', the son concluded.

'Well son, you have given me very good reasons for your failure to marry. Let me however make one point clear to you. You are yourself not perfect. Do not therefore expect to come upon a perfect woman. That fastidiousness of yours is in fact the greatest weakness. Be realistic and get a wife to marry'.

'I accept your counsel father. I shall keep searching for a wife that will bring me happiness'.

He however forgot that happiness in a marriage belongs to more than the wife and the husband. He did not realise what unhappiness he was causing the father. In the end, the father died. But just before his last breath, he called the son and told him: 'Dear son, I am dying. There is no need for you to marry'.

And the son when he also died, was still a bachelor.[60]

The narrative would most suit the marriageable young men and women. The men are advised against being too choosy and idealistic. They must accept that perfection is a puppet dream. Human beings have their weaknesses and that perhaps underlines the need to marry. There is no one who has all the admirable qualities. We must learn to tolerate others' shortcomings.

To the females the message is less direct. The story lists the discrediting traits that discourage potential husbands e.g. gossiping, inanity, quarrelsomeness, gluttony, extravagance and thievery. These are not the only vices but a good summary. The story then asks for an introspection in an effort to be more accommodating.

At the subtler level we see the societal concern for marriage. It is an institution that is cherished and looked forward to as a promise of continuity of the human race. Remaining unmarried is a social disgrace not only to the individual, but to the whole family and society. In fact, among the Luo a spinster or bachelor is buried like a child.

Quite often tales end with explicit statements of their morals in the form of proverbs, dictums, or aphorisms. But sight must not be lost of the fact that a tale may have more than one didactic point to make.

Cultural Records

The culture of a people is the totality of their way of life. It includes religion, beliefs and customs, practices, music, literature, attitudes, philosophies – everything that goes to make the society. By being didactic, the stories present to us the philosophical essence of the society. How do they look at life issues? What do they value or decry?

Turning to the socialisation, we are exposed to the artistic ways the society keeps itself sane by relaxation and creative engagement. It is all part of human life to socialise and engage in recreation. This stems from the physiological need for activity and rest.

The content of the oral traditions of a people epitomise the foundations of that group. The tales on religion, creation and supernature give the religious foundations of a group. Biographies and historical tales present the mundane landmarks in what is the society today. Through the traditional heroes we appreciate what the society admires.

Let us take an example of the Maasai narrative to analyse the cultural content.

The Twins of the Drum

Once upon a time there lived a man who had two wives. One of the wives was barren and the other one had very many children. The man lived with his wives for very many years.

The barren woman was unhappy because she did not have children of her own. She did most of the work in her house, since she had no one to assist her. Compared with her co-wife, she had fewer domestic duties to keep her at home. She was assigned the task of herding and watering the flock by her husband. These are chores which are normally performed by men and barren women.

As time went by, the barren woman felt very bitter, neglected and lonely. She became extremely jealous of the other woman. After a while, the fertile woman gave birth again, this time to twin boys. The barren woman became even more green with jealousy. She worked out a plan to run down the image of the co-wife in the home and in the neighbourhood.

One night when their mother was heavily asleep, the barren woman took the twins and cut off their fingers to let out blood, which she smeared around the mouth of their mother. It was going to seem obvious that the fertile woman had eaten her own children. The barren woman grabbed the twins, put them in a drum and dumped the drum into the river. She went around the village and told everyone she met about how her co-wife had eaten her children. Everyone was bewildered.

The mother of the twin children tried desperately to explain to the incredulous neighbours what had actually happened, but no one would believe her, especially on seeing the blood on her mouth and failing to trace the twins. The husband too believed the story of his barren wife; his fertile wife was declared a cannibal. He beat the bereaved woman until she could cry no more. As if this was not enough, he sentenced her to lifetime herding of donkeys, a menial job normally performed by children and labourers.

Meanwhile, the drum containing the twin brothers remained afloat on the river, season in season out. It was swept away by gentle current to another country, until one day, elders who sat under cool shade by the river deliberating on affairs of the clan, noticed the drum as it was swept adrift to the river bank.

"That drum is mine!", one of them said, agitated.

"Whatever is inside is mine!" another one burst out.

The elders scampered to the drum, and holding it by both hands removed it from the water.

They plucked it open and pulled out the frail twin boys. The drum and its contents were shared out equally amongst the anxious rescuers. The elder who had been given the share of the twin boys quickly brought them to his home, nursed them until they became big strong warriors. They were nicknamed "the twins of the drum".

As they grew into big men, the twins became restless. They were told many stories about how they had been rescued. They grew curious and anxious. They wanted to know their country of origin. Eventually, they said to each other: "Look, let us gather some presents and search for our motherland".

They set out on the homebound journey. It was a journey of search, in the cause of which they encountered a famished, sickly woman who was tending healthy rotund donkey. They had never seen a woman herding donkeys. They stopped and asked her, "Mother, why are you herding donkeys? Where have the children gone?" They showed her the remains of their fingers which had been chopped short by a cruel barren woman and repeated the story which the people in the strange land had told them. On discovering that she was their mother, they were overjoyed. The young men dressed their mother in new garments and set out for the village. They left the donkeys in the field.

When the villagers saw the "donkey woman", as she had come to be known, all dressed up, they were mesmerised. "Has the donkey woman found the sons she had eaten?" they wondered. A council of elders was convened. It was established that the young warriors were the sons of the old man. He raved in shame and pain and humiliation when he remembered the way he had punished his innocent wife. He threatened to kill his barren wife but his sons advised him to let the barren woman do the donkey job. She was sentenced to herd donkeys for the remainder of her life. The old man, his wife and the twin sons then lived happily ever after.[61]

From this tale are certain things about the Maasai culture. First is that they practised polygamy. And secondly is their regard for children and fertility. Children in the family bring a sense of completeness. As is characteristic of most, if not all African communities, a woman is regarded so by proof of her fertility. It is the crowning glory. That is why the barren woman is despised and mistreated. By being unable to bear, she is more or less like a man. Notice that this is emphasised by the job she is given: "chores which are normally performed by men and barren women".

We see the same justice meted out to the alleged cannibal. She is made to herd donkeys, a chore for "children and labourers". The judicial system is such that follies are punished by manual labour and adherence of the condemned to their fate. What strikes us is the proportionality of the punishment to the crime of the evil woman. Why is she not condemned to death? Probably the capital penalty does not exist in the culture or otherwise the death of children does not warrant that. Anyhow the punishment lets the woman live on until the truth is established.

What about the donkeys and cattle? We know that the Maasai are historically a nomadic pastoralist group. Living in a climatically hostile environment, the donkey is an asset. Donkeys are hardy animals that survive on scanty pasture and minimal water. They can also be used for a variety of domestic chores.

Turning to the larger community we see the humanity of the elders, when they receive and bring up the children. It is possible that in some groups such a strange find as the twins would be treated differently, probably by having them killed. The elders's act tells us that the community adopts a cautionary approach to events and lets them unfold.

And so we get an insight into aspects of Maasai culture as an illustration of the cultural import of narratives.

CONCLUSION

In the foregoing chapters we have explained the various aspects of the narrative genre. Narratives have passed from the ancient to the present generations by word of mouth. They have survived the test of time because of the universality of their messages across time and boundaries. Thus we still find them relevant and adoptable to our experiences today.

As time passes on, they still have to be passed down to our descendants. Noticeably, this may not be solely through the oral word. Literacy and other aspects of modern life come in to aid the preservation and further transmission of the narratives. For instance, several anthologies have been published and more will. They are a relatively more permanent record of these valuable assets. Secondly, they also make the corpus available to more than the mother community. The audio-tape and cinema are other facilities used to capture the oral arts for preservation and use in the future.

While that is true, the narratives themselves are getting changed. They are getting infused with concepts from the present world so that they make meaning to the present generation. For example, I got this story from *The Sunday Nation* of 25th February, 1990. It talks about iron sheets, magistrates, e.t.c., ideas which belong to the modern world.

Hare Gets Top Post After Tricking Ambitious Hippo
by Henry A. Emutsuru

Once upon a time there lived two animals, Hippopotamus and Porcupine. They were great friends.

One day Porcupine was standing on the river bank. He was talking to Hippo who was floating on the water near the bank.

Porcupine told Hippo: "Look, you can be the magistrate in the water and I can be the magistrate on the land".

"If we are both magistrates, then we can do what we like. We can make the little animals and the small nile perch do everything we want."

Porcupine and Hippo both laughed and thought that they were alone. They did not know that little Hare was listening to everything they said. He was hiding in the bush at the bank just next to where Porcupine was standing.

"I must stop this", thought Mr. Hare. "I don't want Porcupine to be the magistrate on the land".

He decided to play a trick on the two animals. When Porcupine had gone away for a while, Hare got a long rope and went down the river.

"Mr. Hippo", he called. "Could you help me please?"

"What is the matter?" asked Hippo swimming towards the bank.

"My vegetable pot that I kept under my cave has stuck in the mud", said Hare, "and I can't lift it up because it is completely covered with mud".

"What can I do about it?" Hippo asked.

"I will tie this rope around the pot and then the remaining rope I will tie around you," said Hare.

Hippo soon accepted. He didn't know Hare had dug the ground and taken a pot of bees and put it in the hole, then covered it with a piece of iron sheet with some mud on it.

A little while after Hare had finished tying Hippo, Porcupine also arrived. He also agreed to help Hare in getting out the pot.

So Hare took the rope and tied Porcupine by the left. He then moved far and shouted: "Pull, pull".

As they pulled the pot into pieces, the bees came out at high speed and the animals were stung to death. Hare therefore became the magistrate of the land.[62]

At another level, we see the application of oral narratives in the writing of both creative and analytical works. A classic example is the novel *The Strange Bride*[63] by Grace Ogot. This is a novel based on the Luo myth rationalising the origin of digging. The narrative has it that initially there was a sacred hoe which was used to strike the ground only once and then it dug itself afterwards. But then one time an impudent woman decided to strike the ground with it more than once. In anger then, God decreed that man should dig the ground to grow food. The novel is woven around the motif in what attests to the indebtness of written to oral literature.

By and large therefore, we can only conclude that our oral literature is moving ahead with the times and adopting new perspectives.

NOTES

1. Rose Mwangi, *Kikuyu Folktales*, Kenya Literature Bureau: Nairobi, 1982 (3rd edition), p. 3.
2. In the book *Oral Literature: A School Certificate Course*, by S. K. Akivaga and A. B. Odaga, published by Heinemann, 1982.
3. In the book *African Oral Literature for Schools*, by Jane Nandwa and Austin Bukenya, published by Longman, 1983.
4. Naomy Kipury, *Oral Literature of the Maasai*, Heinemann: Nairobi, 1983.
5. Ruth Finnegan, *Oral Literature in Africa*, Oxford University Press: Nairobi, 1970, p 328.
6. Ibid.
7. Nandwa and Bukenya, op.cit. p. 43.
8. Akivaga and Odaga, op.cit. p. 20.
9. Kipury, op.cit. p. 16.

10. B. Onyango-Ogutu and A. A. Roscoe, *Keep My Words*, Heinemann: Nairobi, 1974, p. 43-4.
11. A. B. Odaga, *Thu Tinda*, Uzima Press: Nairobi, 1980, p. 135-6.
12. Kipury, op.cit. p. 112-3.
13. W. M. Kabira and K. Mutahi, *Gikuyu Oral Literature*, Heinemann: Nairobi, 1988, p. 100-2.
14. The full version of the story can be read in Luo language from A. W. Mayor's *Thuond Luo*, Anyange Press: Kisumu, 1938, p. 29-33.
15. Kipury, op.cit. p. 39-40.
16. Ibid. p. 29-30.
17. Lucy W. Kibera, *Children's Wisdom Stories*, Kenya Literature Bureau: Nairobi, 1985, p. 57.
18. Finnegan, op.cit. p. 364.
19. Kabira and Mutahi, op.cit. p. 5-7.
20. Jan Knappert, *Myths and Legends of the Congo*, Heinemann: London, 1971, p. xiii.
21. Mwangi, op.cit. p. 7.
22. Finnegan, op.cit. p. 322.
23. Ibid.
24. Knappert, op.cit. p. xiii.
25. Kabira and Mutahi, op.cit. p. 73-6.
26. Finnegan, op.cit. p. 375.
27. Ibid.
28. Ibid, p. 380.
29. Ibid.
30. Ogutu and Roscoe, op.cit. p. 26.
31. Odaga, op.cit. p. 98-101.
32. Kipury, op.cit. p. 77-9.
33. Odaga, op.cit. p. 53-68.
34. Finnegan, op.cit. p. 328-9.
35. Ogutu and Roscoe, op.cit. p. 129-133.
36. Akivaga and Odaga, op.cit. p. 53-62.
37. Ogutu and Roscoe, op.cit. p. 100-2.
38. Ibid, p. 80-82.
39. Kabira and Mutahi, op.cit. p. 49-51.
40. Mwangi, op.cit. p. 80-5.
41. Kipury, op.cit. p. 46-8.
42. Ibid, p. 59-61.
43. Ibid, p. 62-3.
44. Ibid, p. 49-52.
45. Ibid, p. 454-8.
46. Anthony J. Barrett, *Turkana Way of Life*, New World Printers: Nairobi, 1988, p. 88.
47. Ogutu and Roscoe, op.cit. p. 100-7.
48. Kipury, op.cit. p. 49-52.
49. Ogutu and Roscoe, op.cit. p. 108-114.
50. Kipury, op.cit. p. 97-100.
51. Kabira and Mutahi, op.cit. p. 78-81.
52. Mwangi, op.cit. p. 114.

53. Ibid, p. 130-1.
54. Kabira and Mutahi, op.cit. p. 60-2.
55. Odaga, op.cit. p. 36-41.
56. Kipury, op.cit. p. 62-3.
57. Ibid, p. 86-7.
58. Ibid, p. 74-6.
59. A version of the same story is published in A. B. Odaga's *Thu Tinda*, as 'In Search of a Perfect Wife', p. 96-8.
60. Kipury, op.cit. p. 101-3.
61. 'The Sunday Nation', February 25, 1990. p. 21.
62. *The Strange Bride* published by Heinemann Kenya Ltd, 1989.

BIBLIOGRAPHY

1. Achebe, C. *Things Fall Apart*, Heinemann: London, 1958.
2. Adagala, K. and Kabira, W. (ed). *Kenyan Oral Narratives*, Heinemann: Nairobi, 1985.
3. Akivaga, S. K. and Odaga, A. B. *Oral Literature: A School Certificate Course*, Heinemann: Nairobi, 1982.
4. Barra, G. *1000 Kikuyu Proverbs*, Kenya Literature Bureau: Nairobi, 1987.
5. Barrett, J. A. *Turkana Way of Life*, New World Printers: Nairobi, 1988.
6. Beier, U. (ed). *African Poetry*, Cambridge University Press: 1966.
7. Castle, A. B. *Quotes and Anecdotes*, St. Paul Publications: Bombay, 1983.
8. Chesaina, C. *Oral Literature of the Kalenjin*, Heinemann: Nairobi, 1991.
9. Delano, O, Isaac. *Yoruba Proverbs*, Oxford University Press; Ibadan, 1966.
10. Egudu, R. and Nwoga, D. *Igbo Traditional Verse*, Heinemann: London, 1973.
11. Farsi, S. S. *Swahili Sayings I*, Kenya Literature Bureau: Nairobi, 1982.
12. Finnegan, R. *Oral Literature in Africa*, Oxford University Press: Nairobi, 1970.
13. Kabira, W. M. and Mutahi, K. *Gikuyu Oral Literature*, Heinemann: Nairobi, 1988.
14. Kibera, L. W. *Children's Wisdom Stories*, Kenya Literature Bureau: 1985.
15. Kipury, N. *Oral Literature of the Maasai*, Heinemann: Nairobi, 1983.
16. Knappert, J. *Myths and Legends of the Congo*, Heinemann: London, 1971.
17. Malo, S. *Sigend Luo Maduogo Chuny*, Lake Publishers and Enterprises: Kisumu, 1989.
18. Mapanje, J. and White, L. *Oral Poetry in Africa*, Longman: New York, 1983.
19. Massek, A. O. and Sidai, J. O. *Wisdom of Maasai*, Transafrica Publishers: Nairobi, 1974.
20. Major, A. W. *Thuond Luo*, Anyange Press: Kisumu, 1938.
21. Mbiti, J.S. *Akamba Stories*, Oxford University Press: Nairobi, 1966.
22. Mboya, P. *Luo Kitgi Gi Timbegi*, Anyange Press: Kisumu, 1938.
23. Mirimo, A.K.L. *Luhyia Sayings*, Oxford University Press: Nairobi, 1988.
24. Mwakasaka, C.S. *The Oral Literature of the Banyankyusa*, Kenya Literature Bureau: Nairobi, 1978.
25. Mwangi, R. *Kikuyu Folktales*, Kenya Literature Bureau: Nairobi, 1982.
26. Mwikali K. and Coughlin P. *Barking You'll Be Eaten*, Phoenix Publishers: Nairobi, 1988.
27. Nandwa, J. and Bukenya, A. *African Oral Literature for Schools*, Longman: Nairobi, 1983.
28. Odaga, A.B. *Poko Nyar Migumba*, Foundation Books Ltd: Nairobi, 1978.
29. Odaga, A.B. *Yesterday's Today*, Lake Publishers: Kisumu, 1991.
30. Odaga, A. B. *Thu Tinda*, Uzima Press: Nairobi, 1980.
31. Ogot, Grace. *Ber Wat*, Anyange Press: Kisumu, 1981.
32. Ogot, Grace, *The Strange Bride*, Heinemann: Nairobi, 1989.
33. Ogutu, B. O. and Roscoe, A. A. *Keep My Words*, Heinemann: Nairobi, 1974.
34. Okombo, O. and Nandwa, J. (ed) *Reflections and Theories in Oral Literature*, KOLA: Nairobi, 1992.
35. Omtata, O. *Lwanda Magere*, Heinemann: Nairobi, 1991.
36. P'Bitek, Okot, *Acholi Proverbs*, Heinemann: Nairobi, 1985.
37. P'Bitek, Okot, *African's Cultural Revolution*, Macmillian: Nairobi, 1973.
38. P'Bitek, Okot, *Artist the Ruler*, Heinemann: Nairobi, 1986.

39. P'Bitek, Okot, *Horn of My Love*, Heinemann: Nairobi, 1974.
40. Schipper, M. *Source of All Evil*, Phoenix Publishers: Nairobi, 1992.
41. Vansira, Jan. *Oral Tradition as History*, East African Educational Publishers: Nairobi, 1992.